IT'S NEVER TOO LATE TO DATE

Too many women in their 50s and beyond have given up on ever meeting Mr. Practically Perfect. But a small inner voice wonders, "Will I always have to eat alone and go to bed with a book?" Responding to that voice, the authors' inspiring message is, "It's never too late. We did it. So can you. Here's how!"

Shirley and Howard's Rx's For Dating and Mating After 50

By Shirley Friedenthal and Howard Eisenberg

ASJA Press
New York   Bloomington

It's Never Too Late to Date
Shirley and Howard's Rx's For Dating and Mating After 50

ASJA Press
An imprint of iUniverse, Inc.

For Information address:
iUniverse
1663 Liberty Drive
Bloomington, IN 47403
www.iuniverse.com
1-800-Authors (1-800-288-4677)

ISBN: 978-1-4401-1378-9 (sc)

Printed in the United States of America

iUniverse rev. date: 02/17/09

Contents

"I never in a million years thought I'd be dating in my seventies."

--Elizabeth Taylor

Introduction

BE MY VALENTINE
(But not if you're over 50)

The author of a New York Times Sunday Magazine piece not long ago on the wonderful world of dating interviewed the heads of three popular dating services. Not one word of thousands acknowledged the possibility that a woman over 50 (and certainly not 60) might consider dating. Indeed, the writer seemed stuck in the 1940s radio soap opera days of "The Romance of Helen Trent," whose announcer dramatically intoned, "Can a woman 35 or over still find romance?" Or words to that effect. In ignoring women 50 and older, the Times writer seemed to be saying, "Sorry, Helen. No way. And don't forget to tell your girlfriends."

At about the same time, a lengthy Newsweek cover story devoted to "Sex and the Single Boomer," subtitled "The New World of Midlife Romance," was equally oblivious to life beyond 50. I, for one, was hugely annoyed. Did the editors believe women my age can't go on a date without a nurse's aide and a walker?

I've given a lot of thought to the long-distance loneliness of women like myself whose 50th or 60th birthdays are history and who, for one reason or another, are flying solo. Usually not by choice. I know a lot of lovely women in their 60s and 70s, and many still lively in their 80s and beyond, who have found or would love to find someone to love and be loved by. This book, beginning with my 64-year-old mother's successful makeover and continuing with my story and those of others, is for them. To tell them flat out that (flourish of trumpets!), " It's never too late to date."

Dating books crowd so many shelves at Barnes & Noble that they are almost a library in themselves. They're practical. They're chock full of advice. But almost all speak to the well-under-40 crowd. Only a handful give a polite nod to women in their 50s, and, as for practical dating and make-over counseling, if you're 60 or above, you're the Invisible Woman. There's a disturbing void there that needs filling, and "It's Never Too Late to Date," offering age-appropriate Rx's, is determined to fill it.

Meanwhile, back at the ranch, men, too, are riding alone and lonesome. My co-author searched for three years and had 110 names and phone numbers in his little black book before he found love after 60. (Okay, after 70.) He had just about abandoned hope of meeting anyone who could even begin to measure up to his extraordinary wife of 48 years when his computer announced, "You've got mail." And, suddenly, there I was.

I didn't find love-after-60 overnight either. But it helped that I was born with a practical streak as wide as a Los Angeles freeway. After my husband's death, I systematically answered personals ads in assorted periodicals ("I'm exactly the woman your ad describes," worked really well), registered for e-dating, and even paid a hefty fee to a private dating company (because, hey, this was an investment in the rest of my life) that promised "18 carefully pre-screened and perfect dates in 18 months."

E-dating won. So, I'm happy to report, did Howard and I. Affection and companionship are once more a part of our lives, and I'd like to pass on what we've learned -- from our experiences and from the wisdom of scores of women and men we've met and hundreds we're meeting in senior dating workshops we lead. There's enough happiness to go around. We'd like to help spread it.

It's important. AARPers and their older sisters and brothers are apparently going to be around -- and, in many cases, lonely – a long time. At any age, two's company. One's a hermit. Said hermit may have more peace and quiet, but he's also, -- or so a recent Swedish study of 1,500 men and women tells us -- at a 50 percent greater risk of Alzheimer's than others in midlife who were either married or lived with a significant other.

Now there's a fact worth casually dropping on your next date. You might mention, too (just check out your morning paper's obituary page) that most of us can expect to live 15 to 25 years longer than our parents and grandparents who, at 65, were rapidly approaching their expiration dates. That's an incredible gift, so senior or pre-senior, female or male, you don't want to be that unfortunate hermit. And, guys, there's clearly a lot to be said, longevity-wise, for being a lady's home companion.

Hollywood is a little slow on that uptake. Rarely does a film depict older Americans experiencing the call of the wild -- one of the few exceptions being Jack Nicholson's sharing a hot tub with a less than nubile grandma in "About Schmidt." Of course, that scene was played for laughs because, well, could sex between consenting seniors possibly be taken seriously?

Never mind. Senior women are no laughing matter. Today, thanks in part to a patchwork of medical and anatomical miracles, there are more than 20 million of us in the U.S. -- single, largely able-bodied, and 50 or over -- ready for action. Happily, there are more men than there used to be, too – well over 15 million and growing. (And if that's a little vague, it's because the phone listed for the Special Populations Staff of the U.S. Census Bureau must have suffered a budget cut. It "is out of service at this time.")

That gives unattached women a larger pool of men to swim with than at any time since the Age of Methuselah. But because there are, as always, millions more women than men, women have to think and act smarter to make a meaningful connection. Even 2-1 odds (which is what they rise to at 85) aren't bad though. (There are 95 men for every 100 women aged 45-54, 91 per 100 women 55-64, 83 men per 100 women in the next decade, and 70 per 100 women aged 75-84.) The good news is that since at least half of all available women have made themselves unavailable by giving up, your odds at any age over 50 are darned good. Plus: this book's Rx's can help.

Karl Menninger defined happiness as something to do, someone to love, and something to look forward to. Working women always have something to do -- often too much. For a single retired senior woman, bridge and the monthly book club can be that "something to do." A Metropolitan Museum of Art or an Elderhostel cruise can be the "something to look forward to." But in the quiet moments of the night when she turns out the light and turns over on her pillow, a woman can't help thinking how wonderful it would be if she had "someone to love." Well you can, and we want to help you.

Think about this. These days, millions of men in their 50s and beyond, who in generations past enjoyed nothing but their fantasies, are going out on dates with carefully wrapped Viagra tablets slipped into their wallets – just as, when they were wishful-thinking 16-year-olds, they secreted condoms. Like the teenagers they once were, they can't wait to use them. With, of course, their doctors' consent.

Seneca spoke of declining age as "an incurable disease," and La Rochefoucauld described it as "a tyrant which forbids the pleasures of youth on pain of death." (They didn't tell us. We found that in a book of quotations.) How unhappily true then. How happily untrue, now. Today the prime of life is followed by the cream of life, and those who choose to lap it up instead of sitting around watching TV and bemoaning their cholesterol counts can have the time of their lives. If they're comfortable with the idea, and not everyone is, dating -- sometimes followed by loving, consensual, occasionally viagrafied sex -- can make that time richer and more rewarding. The song says it: "Hey, everybody. Let's have some fun. You only live once, and then it's done."

We have a choice: one foot in the grave (figuratively, not immediately) or two feet on the dance floor. The dreariest years of our lives, or the happiest. This book can help you choose. Every week, another 25,000 of us face the Big 60 and wonder, "Is this all there was?" Well, there can be a lot more.

Remarkably, some 48,000 Americans celebrated 100th birthdays in 2001, and with improved life styles (and such wild cards as the genetically engineered Klotho Gene already adding one-third to the life spans of laboratory mice), we are a population on steroids. We're less focused on meeting a mate, but many of us (though we may not confide this to our friends) would like nothing better. We crave companionship and affection.

This book aims to see that you get it. And it's nice to know that for every lonely woman helped, it will help a lonely man.

MAKE THIS YOUR THEME SONG

It's never too late to date
It's never too late to change your life
To move from okay to great
To totally change your fate.
Dating's not just for teens
Not just for 30-somethings
If you're still full of beans
Hey, why not make the scene?
You can fall in love at 50…or 60…or 80
Methuselah had girlfriends when he was 802
It's no fun to sleep alone, or dine alone in a restaurant
So find a man who's perfect – or almost perfect for
you
Find yourself a partner and bid loneliness adieu.
It's never too late to date
It's never too late to change your life
It's never ever too late
To find a significant mate.

Chapter One
MINNIE'S MAKEOVER

My mother was my first attempt to play matchmaker. She was also proof positive that it's never too late to date. At 63, with "loser" written across her ample bosom in capital letters, Minnie was an unlikely candidate for a first date or a second husband. But after my father died, ending a long marriage in which they had been as ill-matched as two left shoes, I revisited my girlhood home. My mission: to try to help my mother find the happiness she'd never had in a loveless marriage arranged by my domineering grandmother.

I found Minnie seated in front of the TV munching potato chips. There, wearing a faded housecoat, she remained during most of my visit. It was clear that she felt that her life was over, that the odds of any man falling in love with her at her age were about the same as of winning the Irish Sweepstakes. I disagreed. I turned off the TV.

"Your life here is boring," I declared. (I guess it was in the genes. I could be pretty domineering, too.) "Come to New York. I'll help you find a man and get a life." "Find a man? Who'd be interested in me? Look at me in these *shmattes*. What man would give me a second glance?"

"We'll get rid of the old clothes," I said. "Once I fix you up, men are going to like you. You're funny. You play the piano. You sing 'God Bless America' better than Kate Smith. Like you? Men are going to love you." Minnie didn't believe me. "Who," she repeated, "would

1

want an old lady like me?" But she liked New York. And she liked the idea of spending more time with her grandchildren. "Okay," she said, "It's crazy, but I'll come."

My sisters thought I was crazy, too. But they've thought that my whole life. Anyway, I had a plan. The Salvation Army cleaned out Minnie's pots, pans, and furniture -- including the TV set -- and she came to New York to live with my young family. She loved the Bronx and the tempting ethnic delicacies she could buy there -- the crusty oniony potato knishes, the savory corned beef and pastrami -- but I wouldn't let her eat them. I put her on a small-portions-only diet, and proscribed her beloved potato chips and Baby Ruth chocolate bars. "You're starving me!" she declared. To which I replied, "If you want to get a man, you've got to lose some weight."

It took three months, constant vigilance, and a lot of will power Minnie didn't know she had. Gradually, overweight turned into pleasingly plump. At 4'11," she would never look like a Ziegfield Girl, but with 20 pounds subtracted, she cast a shadow less like a motorcycle and more like a bike.

Minnie's grandson Michael, 14, now joined the team. After menopause, when testosterone overwhelms slowly diminishing female hormones, many older women tend to grow unsightly hair on their chins and upper lips. Minnie was one of those unfortunates. She was no circus Bearded Lady, but neither was her chin hair a selling point. Electrolysis was expensive, but the job had to be done. Michael worked out. His strong fingers plucked her like, well, like a chicken.

Minnie's smile was next. Her ill-fitting dentures occasionally slipped in mid-sentence. To our family, the slip was endearing. For a suitor, the slip could be fatal. I took her to a reliable dentist (my sisters Ann and Frieda chipped in) and two weeks later Minnie had a glamorous new set of dentures and a sparkling non-slip smile. The one thing I couldn't do was stop her from biting her nails.

Next step was the beauty parlor for hair tinting and a face-framing perm, and we followed that by thumbing department store dress racks until Michael's closet (he shared his bedroom with his grandmother) was packed with Minnie's new dresses. Then we replaced her black granny shoes with sandals. When we were finished, my mother, with the carriage of a queen after weeks of reminders to "Stand up straight!", smiled at herself in the full-length mirror and said, "Umm, I haven't looked this good since my wedding day."

Minnie was now ready for prime time. What she saw in the mirror renewed her belief in herself. Her personality went from passive to positive. She joined the local community center and made new friends. One of them helped her write, with much girlish giggling, responses to three widower-seeks-wife ads in "The Forward." The phone rang three times. Feeling like Cinderella, Minnie went out with all three callers. "Look at me! Three dates!" she exclaimed with a swish of her skirts, and each time came back smiling. "Two of them I really like," she said, "but I'd like you to meet them."

Harry was charming, intelligent, kindly, and looked at her fondly and with genuine pleasure. When my sisters and their families came to meet him, there wasn't a negative vote in the crowd. A few months later, they were married. Minnie moved to his apartment in Queens, and when he died five years later, she told me through her tears that they had been the best five years of her life. "Not only that," she confided. "I never knew that sex could be so wonderful."

What I did for my mom, you can, following Shirley and Howard's Rx's, do for yourself. And if you need chin hairs plucked, I'll lend you Michael.

Chapter Two
HOW SHIRLEY MET HOWARD

And now a case history. Ours. Besides offering further evidence that it's never too late to date, it illustrates how wrong first impressions can be, how badly things can go on a first date, and the importance of patience and a sense of humor because -- we are proof positive -- even the worst date can turn into a great ongoing relationship.

Meet the authors: Shirley and Howard. She a merry widow. He a depressed widower. Read on as they become a couple, discover great sex (though, of course, not right away), become OOs (One and Only's), and decide to invite the entire mature singles world to the party by writing this book. Its purpose: to help you connect with that special stranger who, upon entering the room, will spike your temperature and purse your lips into an involuntary and at least semi-ecstatic, "OO!"

SHIRLEY: We met on J-Date. My son, Michael, a computer whiz who works for Apple, helped set up my profile, and since he's a man, I let him choose the photo. "This side view is great, Mom," he said. "It showcases your, er, bosom." Men, he assured me (like I was born yesterday) love bosoms. From the number of e-mails I found in my mailbox the next day, that goes double for older men.

I went out with four or five of them. The dentist lost me when, delivering me to my door after our date, he attempted a soulful French connection, opening his mouth so wide I was afraid a train would come out. I connected him with my front door. Another, a really nice man, shocked me when he phoned exuberantly after our second date. "Shirley," he said, "I love you. You're the woman of my dreams. I couldn't sleep last night. I want you to meet my children. I've told them I'm going to marry you. Let's set a date." He went on and on, leaving me -- and this is unusual -- speechless. He was a lovely man, but alarmingly impulsive. Plus, I was not about to remarry. I stopped taking his phone calls.

In front of a Rodin bronze in the Metropolitan Museum, a third date suddenly turned, swept me back over his arm, declared, "I can't resist you!" and kissed me passionately. It was grandly romantic, but that, and some of his other moves, seemed, well, a bit slick and premeditated. That was his last date.

Then, along came Howard. His profile admitted to 72 (like most E-daters, he'd subtracted a few years) but he looked younger. In a snapshot from a New Zealand vacation, he wore a kind of rancher's hat and cradled a lamb in his arms. (It could have been a goat. I didn't look that hard. It wasn't the one I was dating.) There was something about his smile. Him I wanted to meet.

HOWARD: Shirley doesn't believe me -- maybe you won't either -- but, though I found her photo interesting, I didn't especially notice her, well, her upper body. (I'd be lying if I claimed not to have noticed it since.) We met on West 45th St. in Manhattan where we'd agreed to go for a snack before a show. In the three years since the death of a very special wife, I'd had dozens of dead-end dates. So I was lost in thought and prepared for the worst as I walked east toward the theatre, wearing the black beret that was to identify me. Suddenly, an attractive woman walking west confronted me. "A beret," she said. "You must be Howard."

SHIRLEY: We crossed the street and went into a little Italian restaurant. I ordered a shrimp cocktail. "Shrimp cocktail?" he exclaimed, as though I had kicked a baby in the head. "What," I asked, "is wrong with shrimp cocktail?" When it arrived, I proceeded to enjoy it, totally unaware that crustaceans like shrimp, no matter how tasty, are on the Old Testament's short list of forbidden foods, and Howard takes the O.T. very seriously. Well, how was I supposed to know? But I would have ordered them anyway. It's my stomach.

HOWARD: Well, people's choices are a matter of free will, and I certainly have no right to tell someone what to eat or not eat. I don't know why I said that. I was just, well, surprised.

SHIRLEY: So our first date got off to a bad start. Then it got worse. When the subject of our former spouses came up, tears appeared in Howard's eyes. "I'm sorry," he said, blotting them. "It happens whenever my wife's name comes up. My first date after she died was with a psychotherapist. She told me that when her marriage broke up, she took to her bed with a bag of popcorn, clicked on the TV, and stayed there two months, sobbing and eating Chinese take-out. She gained 20 pounds. We went to dinner in a little Italian restaurant, and when she asked about Arlene, the tears started flowing. I ran out of pocket tissues, used up the paper napkins on the table, and then got a bunch at the counter. At that point, my date donned her therapist's mantle. 'You,' she declared, 'are not ready for a relationship.'"

Wiping his eyes in another Italian restaurant three years later, Howard still didn't seem ready. After the show, we parted company politely and I never expected to see him again. Next day, when my tennis partner asked me how things had gone, I said flatly, "He's religious. He's depressed. After three years, he's still mourning his wife. And he's not my type."

HOWARD: But I had subscription theatre tickets for the following Wednesday and no one I wanted to take. Shirley was a doctor's widow. A grief counselor had told me that widows and widowers understood each other's losses. Of course, that was only one shrink's opinion. But I telephoned her.

SHIRLEY: I'd been dating other men who seemed more promising candidates -- a doctor, a dentist, an IBM executive, a rancher -- but something about Howard's telephone baritone got to me. And with all his negatives, there was something oddly endearing about him. I heard myself saying, "Okay, it's a date." It was cold in the theater. He slipped off his jacket, wrapped it over my shoulders, and put an arm around me to keep me warm. I liked that.

On our third date, he cabbed me to Grand Central for my ride home to Westchester, and, instead of just dropping me off, walked with me to the train. I liked that, too. And the soft little kiss he gave me at the gate felt good all the way home. But on our fourth date, the tears spilled down his cheeks once more. While handling patient relations in my husband's medical office, I had taken many courses in Rational Therapy. Now, harsh though it might sound, I applied what I'd learned. "Look," I said, "your wife, like my husband, is gone and never coming back. If you think your life is over, go home and end it. If you want to live and you want to see me again, for heaven's sake, stop crying!" He looked stunned. For a long moment, he said nothing. Then, slowly, he said: "You're right."

HOWARD: Call it Rational Therapy. Call it Icewater Therapy. Call it Shirley speaking her mind. She accomplished what three years of mourning and roughly scores of computer dates and fix-ups had failed to do. She brought me to my senses. Our fifth date brought me -- well, read on.

SHIRLEY: We went to a Shakespeare event in Central Park. Not the one in the outdoor arena but further uptown, a kind of guerrilla Shakespeare with the actors moving from one meadow to another and the audience following. Howard's agility impressed me. Sitting on the grass for each scene, then bouncing up to move on for the next one. For a guy in his 70s, this was pretty good. Better than I could do with my jogger's knees. He, I learned, worked out three times a week. Score one for Howard. After the show, we adjourned to his brownstone. It was my first visit, but I had decided to make it one that would test his athleticism in even more memorable ways. I didn't have to make an announcement. I knew. He knew. I was not there to see his kitchen.

HOWARD: I said, "My office downstairs has a futon. All we have to do is figure out how to open it."

SHIRLEY: We did.

Part One
SELF-MOTIVATE

"I feel like a jalopy. I'm losing fenders and hubcaps."
-- Jane Fonda

Rx No. 1:
Want to fly? Flap your wings.

Too many women wait for a man to fall out of the sky into their arms. Unfortunately, except for the rare stunt parachutist who lands off course, that doesn't happen often. So apathy -- sitting and waiting for love without exerting the effort to make it happen -- just may be the number one cause of single woman loneliness.

Consider the robin. Could she fly if she perched apathetically on a tree branch waiting for a favorable breeze? Not likely. Robin knows that if she fails to flap her wings, an earlier bird is going to catch the worm. So with a flick of her feathers, she's airborne.

I know a woman in Colorado who could teach robins a thing or two. When Joyce's husband of 32 years died, she was a long time mourning. But after a year of breakfast-for-one and supper with the six o'clock news, she took a walk in the fresh mountain air one morning, and, meditating as she walked, finally felt ready to move on.

She began her new journey with a silent prayer: "Please, Lord. Open my heart to a new love." Maybe it was the just coincidence, maybe it was her prayer, but a few days later Joyce's landlady rang the bell of her rented condo. "A new man just moved in two doors away from you," she said. "Kinda good-looking, too. Looks to be in his early 60s. Look out for him."

A woman of action, Joyce did look -- out her window. When she saw the tall newcomer stroll to the mailbox, she picked up her mailbox key and strolled nonchalantly after him. Introductions and a 20-minute mailbox chat ensued. In the next few weeks, there were many such conversations as Joyce watched for her neighbor's mailbox visits and timed hers to match his.

"But," she told her son-in-law in some exasperation, "this relationship isn't going anywhere. What do I do now?"

"For heaven's sake," he replied, "this is the 21st century. Ask him out for dinner." But Victor asked first, and a few months later asked a more serious question. "My answer was Yes," says Joyce. "And now only one of us has to go for the mail."

Joyce is a natural-born wing-flapper, but for some of us apathy is a malady difficult to overcome. There were probably a half-dozen other single women fantasizing about Victor as he passed their apartment windows during the first week of his arrival on the condo scene. Unlike Joyce, they were too timid, or too afraid of rejection, to flap their wings.

But don't flap aimlessly. Success starts with a plan. Find yours in the chapters that follow. And relax. There are a lot of lonely men out there waiting for your call. And while you're scouting for Mr. Picture Perfect, you can have the time of your 50-plus life.

MOTIVATION 101

I think that if I really try

I could find myself a guy

But I'm stuck in apathy

In endless hours of TV

I guess that what I need's a nanny

To tell me, "Hey, get off your fanny!"

Rx No. 2:
It's never too late to date.

A little background music here. It didn't seem like it then, but I see now that I was lucky to have a mother too depressed to take care of me. She couldn't be there for me when she took shock treatments, and she couldn't be there for me when she jumped out our second story window, fortunately only fracturing her hip, while I cowered in the closet listening to the wail of the approaching ambulance. (Note: This incident is not James Frey non-fiction fiction. It actually happened.)

It was in those years that I taught myself, "Nothing happens unless you make it happen." So eight years later, at 16, when a 23-year-old boyfriend with his own jewelry store and a new car said he'd do anything I wanted if I'd marry him, I said, "How about driving me to New York?" Which is where, for some reason, I'd always wanted to live. He did -- in those days, 6 1/2 hours each way. Driving down Broadway, I felt like a visiting princess. He parked, we entered the glamorous glittering Automat, I dropped in my nickels for tapioca pudding, ate it slowly savoring every spoonful, and then we turned around and drove home to where I lived on one of the shabbiest streets in the down-at-the-seams textile town of Lawrence, Mass.

It was not, I knew, where I wanted to live my life. It was New York or nowhere, and I knew how to make it happen. So at 18, I withdrew $100 of my hard-earned after-school savings from the bank and invested it in a weekend vacation at Banner Lodge in Connecticut where the boys were -- the New York boys. By weekend's end I had elicited what might be called intensive interest from one from Brooklyn and two from the Bronx. On sequential weekends, I visited their homes, met their parents, and chose the one who, besides being a fine athlete, was handsome and had the best job. And we were married.

Why am I retelling this ancient history? Certainly not because that's the best or only way to pick a husband. I tell it because if you would welcome a man in your life, don't expect a fairy godmother to fit you for a pair of glass slippers, wave her magic wand, and transform a pumpkin into a Lexus to take you to him. To acquire a man, you need to make things happen. To be your own fairy godmother.

Apathy won't make it happen. Rather you've got to think like the 94-year-old Sun Belt widow whose friends said after her husband's funeral, "You're going to be awfully lonely without Charlie. Is there anything we can do to help?"

"Don't worry about me," she replied impishly. "I've already got a new fella. At 94, you can't waste time."

You undoubtedly have more time left than that great-grandma does. Statistically, you're likely to live 20 years longer than your parents did. That's great, but there's a down side. It could mean being alone a long time. Sitting alone with a book at a restaurant table. Going to the movies with the same girlfriends month after month -- friends you're fond of and might invite to stay over of a weekend, but are not inclined to sleep with. Getting your affection from your dog, who wags his tail eloquently when you come home, but can't take you dancing or to dinner or a show.

Some women are comfortable in the single life. For others it's the pits. For a while, friendships substitute for affection. Going out with women friends becomes a kind of stress-free sorority for singles. You meet for mahjong, bridge, or -- just for the auld lang syne fun of it -- for Monopoly. Netflix helps fill your evenings, and you add crossword puzzles to the mix so your brain won't turn to molasses. You read a lot. And you rationalize, "Who needs a man?" even as you muse, "What would it be like to have a warm body beside me at night?"

You'd love to be in love again? Then make it happen. Stop singing, "Those were the days!" and start living these. There used to be a TV show called, "Life Begins at 80." Fifty, 60, 70, or later, your new life -- the one with a new love in it -- begins whenever you decide to begin it. "What man wants a woman my age?" is a loser's question. For every lonely woman, there's a lonely man, and he's probably as discouraged as you about the chances of finding someone to love. So don't think, "Maybe I'll meet someone. On the bus. At the library. At my niece's wedding." Maybe you won't.

If your car stuck in a ditch on a lonely side road, would you sit there and wait until someone came along to rescue you, or would you pull out your cell phone and call AAA? Too many 50-and-overs have been sitting by the side of the road for years when all they needed was to get a move on. Let this book be your AAA. Without annual dues.

Of course, many women find the rut they're stuck in comfortable: "Oh, relationships are too much work. I don't have to dress up. I wear what I want to wear. I don't have to cook what he wants to eat and eat what he wants to eat. Sally's husband goes bananas if she forgets to make coleslaw for his steak. Besides, I've got lots of woman friends, and they're all the company I need."

That's a legitimate point of view. But often it hides the loneliness that lurks beneath the surface and between the lines. Single women do survive better than single men. They're far better at constructing networks of friends who go to dinner and the movies together. And we have a lot more to talk about than men. But many older women remain single because they accept that that's just the way life is going to be from now on.

Men crave affection. They don't stop needing it when they're older. They need and crave it as much or more. Clearly, women do, too, but they're better at accepting friendship in its stead. For many, that's good enough, but it doesn't have to be. It's nice to have someone to put out the garbage, hold hands at the movies with, dance the Golden Oldies with (you can't dance alone), plunge a stuffed toilet. So stay involved in the pursuit of greater happiness.

Marianne did. Three years of caring for her Alzheimer-afflicted husband wore her out, but she still had something left after he died to volunteer for the committee running her high school reunion. Jack's name showed up as she'd secretly hoped it would. She didn't wait for the reunion. She phoned him, they reminisced about the great old days when they'd dated, and three months later they went to the reunion as man and wife. Good things won't happen if you're resigned to being a onesome instead of an awesome twosome for the rest of your life.

Women have reasons other than inertia and apathy for avoiding dating. They don't have to watch a rerun of "Sex in the City" to know that one thing leads to another. The possibility that the "another" could be the bedroom makes some women anxious when they should be eager. Why? "Because," says Regina, "my body hasn't been 18-years-old for 50 years. And who'd want a relic like me?" The answer to that is simple: a perfectly wonderful relic of the opposite sex.

No need to despair if your hourglass figure has gained half an hour. Seek comfort in the results of a recent NPD Group marketing survey which found that over the last 20 years, the percentage of Americans who find overweight people unattractive has dropped steadily from 55 percent to 24 percent. I'm not encouraging you to gain weight. But it's nice to know that three out of four men have presumably reached the good old-fashioned conclusion that "there's more of you to love."

There's undoubtedly more of them to love, too. There are regiments of unattached senior men around, once lightweight, now super-heavyweight, who can't zip up their old Army khakis no matter how hard they suck in their gut. Connect with one of them. Then improve your health and fitness walking into the sunset getting skinny together. Which reminds me of a friend I play bridge with. Alice has been collecting ounces ever since her divorce 15 years ago. "I've got a great idea for an ad," she told me. And a great idea it was. "I'm going to advertise in the Times," she said, "and here's what I'm going to say:

'Obese woman seeks obese man. Let's diet together!'" Now what 250-pound man could resist that?

As so many couples, including the authors of this book, have discovered, it's never too late to fall in love. But falling "in love" isn't the only way to go. Being "in like" with a man you enjoy who becomes your regular and reliable companion isn't bad either. And having a man in your life doesn't mean you have to surrender your other life, the network of women friends who sustained you when, suddenly, after a divorce or a funeral, you were alone. Your new relationship will be healthier and happier if you retain your friends and interests (bridge, tennis, book club), he continues his (poker, mentoring, golf), and you hike, bike, or just plain go to movies and museums together.

Still, reasons for doing nothing -- for not attempting to make things happen – abound. Sometimes it's fear of rejection: "My neck looks like a turkey's. I need to stay away from men with hunting rifles." Or (well, we really do talk this way), "My boobs don't shout, 'Look at me!' the way they did when I was 18." Or, as Victoria told me, "I don't want to take care of an old man." "Vicky," I pointed out, "life is full of surprises. That old man could be taking care of you."

Besides, caretaking's not necessarily a lifetime responsibility. After her husband died, Phyllis lived contentedly with Ezra for seven years. When Alzheimer's struck, and the situation finally became too stressful for her to handle, she called his daughter and said, "Come and get him." Now she just visits.

Rhoda's husband died suddenly seven years ago, and after a decent interval I urged her to look for someone else. "Oh no. Steve was so wonderful. I'll never find anyone like him."

"You won't if you don't try."

"But I loved him so much."

"Steve is gone and you're not."

"Yes. And you know what? I'm tired of eating alone."

She phoned me several weeks later to say she'd registered with a matchmaker service and for computer dating as well. She's optimistic. Ready to make things happen.

A particularly pleasant reason for having a man in your life may be a three-letter word that starts with "s" and ends with "x." But one size doesn't fit all. Anyway, not Shelly. "Who needs sex?" she asked me rhetorically. "When my husband's prostate surgery made him impotent, that's when I was happiest -- with the joy of no sex."

Okay, but that's not true for most of us. Look at the sexy sunshine side. Not only are your kids long since off to college and out of the nest, they're married and busy with kids of their own. You, on the other hand, have time on both hands. When you find that special someone, you won't have to worry about locking the bedroom door or having coitus interrupted by a 4-year-old banging on said door and wailing, "Let me in! Why did you lock the door?" (Try explaining that one with a pillow case wrapped around you.) Thanks to that little blue tablet that's turned older men into supermen, you'll have the best sex since your honeymoon. (Probably a lot better.)

Rosalie doesn't need urging. She took it hard when her husband died of lung cancer. But her sense of humor is still very much alive. When, on a cold winter day, her daughter requested that she take her grandchildren out "for some fresh air," Rosalie asked puckishly, "Can't I just open the window and tell them to inhale?" When Tom, a family friend they'd camped with for many years, dropped in for a visit, Rosalie perked up even more. After a few dates, she visited him for the weekend. Upon her return, Rosalie's daughter noticed a fresh sparkle in her eyes.

Rosalie showed her a note Tom had written, addressed to "my doll, Rosalie." She beamed. "It's a long time," she explained, "since anyone called me doll." Roz understood instinctively what an inscription on the base of a statue in New York's Central Park proclaims in Latin and (fortunately for me) in English, "To lead a better life, lead a different life." Rosalie's life is very different now. Better. That's because she knew instinctively that, no matter what your age, the only thing you get from sitting around waiting for life to happen is creases in your skirt.

"If you want to be a weed, you will be a weed.
If you want to be a flower, you will be a flower."
--Howard

Rx No. 3:
It's never too late to look great.

And never too early to put your best face forward. You don't have to look like Ms. Universe. Not even Ms. Peoria. Just be your new improved self. That self is no longer Sweet Sixteen which, in fact, may be your dress size. But fortunately, you're not the only one who's changed. The man of your daydreams is no longer picture-postcard perfect either.

But even if he isn't, he wants you to be. Since his wife died, his friends have been fixing up my friend, Ed. In the past several months, he's dated a teacher, a nurse, an office manager, and a dentist. Several of them made it clear they'd like to see him again, but Ed politely declined.

"Why?" I asked. "Why didn't you like them? How could you decide so quickly?"

"They just didn't appeal to me."

I knew what he'd say, but I asked anyway: "Why not?"

"Well," he said reluctantly, "I know I'm being superficial. But, truthfully, none of them were really attractive. They were all overweight." He paused, noticing that I'd glanced at his unmistakable paunch. "I know. I know. I can't help it. I just like attractive women."

I talk to a lot of men, and most of them say the same thing. Arlene's father wrote in her public school yearbook, "God's greatest gift is a good woman." And your mother told you it's not what's outside that counts, it's what's inside. They're both right. Substance counts. So does warmth. Intelligence. Sense of humor. Thoughtfulness. Caring. But in choosing a date (and sometimes a mate), most men are as shallow as your bathtub. So when it comes to attracting a man, at least in this day and age, mother doesn't know best. The fact we all have to face is this: looking good helps.

Do bees go for weeds? No, they make a beeline for flowers. But the good news is that though weeds can't get makeovers, we can. So I no longer resemble a Barbie doll (on second thought, who'd want that?) but I, or any other woman, can look better tomorrow than we look today.

You've heard it before. It's worth saying again. You can't love someone else if you don't love yourself. And if your self-esteem runs out of steam, so will your confidence that you can attract a man. Take Inez. "Before my mastectomy," she says, "I was too worried to worry about how I'd look afterward. But afterward, I didn't like my new look one bit, so I arranged for implants – just for me, just for when I look in the mirror. Well, maybe not just for me. I wouldn't be surprised if men admired them, too."

So if you don't like what you see in the mirror, don't break the mirror. Study what's in it. Think about what's wrong with that picture, and then (I'll make helpful suggestions on the pages that follow) develop an action plan to change it. No matter how deep your self-doubt, your cup isn't half-empty. It's just waiting to be filled. Start pouring. Martha, a smartly-dressed well-groomed woman in her mid-60s I met while waiting on a half-price theatre ticket line, has done that ever since she noticed her first wrinkle. "It's paid off," she told me. "I had a date last night with a man 20 years younger than I am. The best part," she laughed, "is *he* thought *he* was older."

We can slow it down, but as it did in those old movie newsreels, time marches on. I no longer look like the shy little girl in my eighth grade graduation picture. Now I look more like her grandmother. But when I get up in the morning, I have a plan. I shower, carefully put on makeup, do my hair, and, even if I'm just going out for my morning walk, dress in something becoming. You never know. Mr. Wonderful Senior could be walking just around the corner. If he is (and even if he isn't) this is no time to be walking the dog in an outfit you should have given to The Salvation Army ten years ago.

Men (surprise!) like attractive women. Ask a dozen men (I did) and 11 out of 12 will put "good looks" or "attractive" at or near the top of their lists of what it takes to get their attention. I berated one of them: "You're 50 pounds overweight. Your tie has gravy spots. You forgot to shave this morning. Just because you're a man, does that give you the right to want to date no one but Miss World?" He didn't have an answer, but he was not prepared to remove "attractive" from the top of his list.

When your house looks weather-worn, you repaint it. Our body is our house, and after 40 or 50 years, most of us need a little touchup. Take care of the fundamentals – hair, skin, eyes. If you've stopped trying to look attractive or seductive, it's time to try again. And don't be dollar-wise and romance-foolish – like patronizing a run-of-the-mall salon where they do an "okay" job, just because it's convenient or $10 cheaper. The hair style you've repeated repeatedly since your senior prom may not fit your face anymore. Your face is your center of attraction, and a poor hairdo surrounding it gets -- guess what -- poor results.

Look around you. Then ask that woman with the great coif where she got it done. Don't ask "How much?" Just do it. A good stylist will size you up ("no short hair for you, it'll make your face look too plump") and transform you from average (or above) to I-can't-believe-I-look-this-good. Too many senior women decide their hair is a pain just above the neck -- too much trouble and expense to care for so they get a mannish cut. Big mistake. Hair is an adornment when properly maintained. It's the picture-frame for your face. Hair that's dull, straggly, or badly cut can ruin the picture. When you look in the mirror when your stylist is done, you should be able to ask, "Gee, who is that?"

Think Rapunzel. Yours may not be shimmering gold and long enough to lower from a tower, but it can help attract your prince. A prison cut won't. When you and your prince repair to the boudoir, you'll want to look your best. You'll want a hairdo that can stand up to serious love-making, so that when the lights go on, the love light in his eyes won't go out. Other than pony- or pigtails, such a coiffeur may not exist. The best solution may be a hair-lifter at bedside to restore your crowning glory as best you can before he opens his eyes. Or sleep with your head under a pillow. (Which might be a great idea for him, too.)

The days of circus Tattooed Ladies are blessedly over, but there is a little something to be said (and, of course, I'll say it) for permanent tattooed-on eyeliner. It saves work, of course. But, more than that, his first look at you in the morning with smeared eyeliner won't suggest that he's acquired a, well, ghoulfriend. If you do tattoo, make sure an experienced dermatologist either does it, or recommends a skilled tattoo artist with lots of credible credentials. Your eyes are too precious to trust to a guy who specializes in anchors, roses, and serpents. But if needles make you nervous (they do me), a good black or dark brown eyeliner will do the job almost as well.

You almost certainly know all this, but it's worth a reminder -- and you can always skip the next several paragraphs. Eyebrow pencil, matching your hair or in the same family, does the essential job of coloring and defining eyebrows. If they need to be shaped and plucked, go to a pro one time. When they need an encore, just do it yourself. Eye shadow on your upper eyelid, using a color that suits your complexion, is a great eye enhancer. If you want to really go Hollywood, match what you're wearing.

Oh yes, don't forget the mascara which, of course, will match your eyeliner, in black, brown, or (not exactly matching, but creating excitement) in almost any color of the rainbow. One more thing. Maybe two. Concealer below the eye performs wonders in making the unflattering puffy circles some of us wear beneath our eyes magically vanish. And I've never tried it, but rumor has it that Preparation H shrinks "bags" as well.

And then there's skin. It's what the whole package is wrapped in, and we want to make it as appealing as possible. Many women aren't aware of this, but dermatologists urge us to wear sun block not just in summer, but 365 days a year. Why? Because, with global warming, cloud cover is less protective and the sun's rays more intense. We need sun block to thwart skin cancer, wrinkling, and dryness. If your block contains a moisturizer, so much the better. If it doesn't, use one.

If you don't buff-puff your face with brown cosmetic (or almost any other) soap when you shower, consider doing it. The puff acts as a kind of cosmetic sandpaper, removing dead skin, stimulating blood supply to the face, and giving you a radiant Danish milkmaid look. I do it mornings in the shower, nights at the sink, especially above the upper lip where lines appear, and around the outside of the eyes.

Did I mention lipstick? Well, I'll mention blush first, which, of course is applied (following the manufacturer's instructions) on nose, chin, and under the cheekbones with brush or fingers. Naturally, it matches your lipstick, which matches your skin. Light skin, light lipsticks. Dark skin, darker shades.

Too many women are still using make-up from "the olden days" -- all wrong for the hue or texture of their skin, and failing to make eyes look bigger or brighter. Try asking the advice of one of the well-trained make-up artists behind the cosmetic counter of a good department store – at a Macy's or Bloomingdale's, for example. Their wares don't come cheap (do cosmetics chemists swirl gold dust into their products?), but your face is not the place to economize. You can go there for free professional advice, but you don't need to keep going back for refills.

I've tested drugstore brands like "Wet and Wild" against the luxury brands and they look and stand up just as well for far less money. So, in case you were getting nervous, there's absolutely no need to spend what starlets at the Golden Globes Awards are reported to lavish on their faces and coifs: an average of $4,000 apiece for that one-night stand.

There's a far less expensive way to go. Sign up with Teenybopper Charm School. Bond with your niece or grand-daughter. Put her in charge of your make-over. Teens read all the beauty magazines, get tips on line, know a lot more than you or I about the latest tricks and products out there. And there is a lot to learn with or without your darling Jessica. Learn from shows on TV, articles in newspapers and magazines, anything that makes sense for you. Start a folder: Man-Catching 101. It's a non-credit course, but you'll be glad you enrolled, and the "A" you get may be a man.

No detail is insignificant when you're reconstructing your persona so that when you look in the mirror, you can believe in yourself and the good things that lie ahead. If you have full (you may suspect too full) breasts, you might want to insert shoulder pads in whatever you're wearing to make them look more proportional. But wear the right bra – choose it carefully – to most effectively flatter them. If your bosom doesn't make a statement, a push-up bra will increase your seductivity score. If you're flat-out flat-chested, consider a padded bra, or – going all out – think about implants and become the most popular single on your block.You always wanted them anyway. (Well, maybe not.)

This will not exactly come as news to you, but men –most men – are as attracted to cleavage as toddlers are to electric outlets and peanut butter and jelly sandwiches. It's primal. It's powerful. It's womankind's greatest weapon since the invention of lipstick. Therapists are at liberty to disagree, but it could be because of golden moments spent long long ago at their mother's breasts. Or for moments missed because she substituted a plastic bottle. One thing you can count on. Their urge doesn't change with age.

Some things do change. As women age and female hormones diminish, hair may grow on chins and upper lips. When I play bridge, I have all I can do to keep from pulling tweezers from my purse and plucking the hairs sprouting from the chin of the woman who just bid three spades. Hers is a male characteristic that turns off many males. And it doesn't have to -- not with tweezers readily available. Or qualified electrolysis technicians -- one of whom an excessively androgenized friend of mine visits every two weeks.

We all have teeth to be whitened, wrinkles to cover up, bags under the eyes (wet teabags used with care, have been known to ameliorate those), pounds where there should be ounces. Some problems respond easily. Some require more work. Some yield to compromises: once smooth peerless skin beneath the chin, for example, that now resembles unpressed shirts. Of course, plastic surgery could smooth out the wrinkles (and your bank account), but I, for one, wouldn't want to be that rare bird who suffers painful complications. I take the knife-free way out: I don a turtleneck shirt and the turkey wattles go out of sight and out of mind.

Brown spots – sometimes referred to as liver spots – are quickly and easily removed by a dermatologist. All-out botoxing of wrinkles?

Liposuction for unloved love handles? I hesitate to recommend such procedures. For one thing, they're darned expensive, and insurance plans – if you're lucky enough to have one -- won't pay a penny. For another, they sometimes go awry. I simply take note of them. Any decision is yours alone.

Exercise is the action piece of your action plan. If you've been putting it off for years, this is not something you're going to enjoy reading. But for both looking good, feeling better, and living longer, fitness is an obligatory habit. And once it becomes a habit, although it will always require self-discipline, it becomes, well, almost fun. If the weather's bad, I walk up and down the stairs. In 20 minutes, that becomes a good sweaty mile. Or I may jog on my treadmill, which goes quickly if you're watching Oprah demolish a dishonest author, or you're reading a good book. Treadmills are too expensive? Not really. You can buy a used one – on the internet or out of the classified -- for less than half the price of a new one. (You'll probably be buying it from a quitter, but don't become one.)

If the weather is good, I do my iPod walk for two or three miles. But you don't need an iPod. A less costly portable CD player works as well. If you're out of shape (if you are, you're not alone), start with a couple of blocks and work your way up. Yes, it sounds boring. A habit you couldn't possibly get into. But for me – first with my old Walkman, more recently with my iPod -- it's become fun with music, and I happen to love music.

Another option: Sign an audio book out of the library and play it on your portable CD or tape player. If you don't have one, invest. As Julie Andrews sang so long ago, a spoonful of sugar helps the exercise medicine go down. Caught up in the narrative of a good book, with your legs on automatic pilot, the time and the miles will pass so quickly that you'll wonder why you haven't caught up on your reading this way all your life. And while you're having fun, your body will firm up as surplus pounds go into meltdown.

Not overnight, of course. You'll have to be consistent -- which if you want to be a Man Magnet, you'll have to be. But exercise is only half the plan.

WEIGHTY MATTERS

The people I
See lifting weights
Don't look like they'd
Be ideal mates.
When making love
And stuff like that
There's no place soft
Enough to pat.

Rx No. 4:
It's never too late to lose weight.

What you eat, and, more important, what you don't eat, is that other half. Add a trivial two pounds a year and pretty soon you're 40 or 50 alarming pounds heavier than when you slipped into your size 6 wedding gown.

The other day I went to a poetry reading at a dingy little bar in Greenwich Village. During a break, I went in search of the ladies' room and found it, in a somewhat unusual architectural configuration, split into two narrow adjacent compartments built not for comfort but for economy of space. As I emerged from one, I encountered a woman in her early 30s eyeing the other space warily. "Is there a problem?" I asked. Inspecting her generous, perhaps 250-pound frame, I could have answered the question myself. But she asked a second one. "Do you think I'll fit?" I didn't want to hurt her feelings. "Oh, no problem," I said. "Just go in sideways." Which, successfully, she did.

Overweight impacts every aspect of our lives, and that certainly includes finding a mate. It was definitely true for the woman in the ladies' room, who came into the bar with a cluster of women friends, most of whom were similarly obese. Hers may not be a fate worse then death (though it may well lead to an early one), but it's not one that most single women I know want for themselves.

31

How to avoid it? Forget all the complicated trick-of-the-month diets and the dubious I-lost-125-pounds in three months claims in TV commercials. Turn your clock back to Weight Watchers, which has not only been around a long time but has been crowned, pound for pound, one of the most successful diet plans ever.

Weight Watchers keeps it simple. No magic incantations, no gimmicks, no complex calculations. You want to reduce your waistline? Reduce your portions. You could sign up for Weight Watchers. With its support group, all-for-one-and-one-for-all atmosphere and calorie-controlled meals, that's not a bad idea. But with a dab of determination and a lot of will power you didn't know you had, you can probably do the deed yourself. But don't be discouraged by relapses. Alcoholics have them. Cocaine addicts have them. And they're actually a good thing if you learn from them. If at first you regain pounds, try try again.

It's easy to postpone the first day of the rest of your life. We all need incentives – from the gold stars once pasted next to Kim, Daniel, Sharon, Michael and the rest of our kindergarten class to the incentive bonus the boss offered for renting the most apartments or selling the most appliances. Want to go for the gold? Try a little visualization. What better incentive could you have than visualizing someone who loves you cuddling with you on the couch as you watch a favorite "Six Feet Under" rerun together?

What's most likely to obliterate that vision? Well, if you can close your eyes and lips to McMuffins for breakfast, it's dinner that's most likely to mess it up. But I've got that one under control even in that most minefield-strewn situation of all: eating out. Under their breath, waiters groan, "Oh, here they come again!" Paying them no mind, Howard and I order one main course and a salad, share them, and go home comfortably full with no need to open our belts a notch. Order less. Eat less.

Restaurant owners, eager to win customers, compete to see who can pile the most food on your plate without its toppling into your lap. If you eat all they serve (and the warm rolls and butter while you wait) you have about as much chance of getting a man in your life as Saddam Hussein has of getting into heaven. So either split your dinner (or lunch) with a friend who shares your interest in losing weight, or draw a line down the middle of your plate, eat half, and take the rest home to be enjoyed as tomorrow's lunch.

Another possibility: order an appetizer or two instead of a main course. (They can be huge, so order one at a time.) Ease into your diet. You could throw away all the cookies, cakes, and ice cream in your kitchen, but another approach would be to say goodbye to them one delicious bite at a time in the coming week and replace them with clementines, berries, apples, and other nutritious, low calorie, naturally sweet substitutes.

This is hard and you deserve a medal. It can come in the form of what my daughter, Leslie, calls her weekly splurge -- a weekend reward day in which you eat anything you want (well, almost anything) without the slightest twinge of guilt or remorse. But that doesn't go for cruises. I avoid them as though there were Nazi U-boats lurking off the starboard bow. I've seen too many fellow passengers walk up the gangplank with a melon belly and waddle down a week later with a watermelon.

I take other measures to keep the fat on the griddle instead of on me. Two or three times a week, I drink a can of chocolate Slim-Fast for breakfast to slenderize my day's calorie count. Occasionally, if I've over-indulged at lunch (and, yes, I confess, occasionally I do), I drink that 180 calories for dinner along with an apple or a nectarine. Not as punishment. It's delicious and they've reduced the sugar by half (though 17 grams is still much higher than it should be), and it leaves me feeling satisfied. And virtuous.

This is not to say that, if you're in a larger dress size than you'd like to be in, that yours is a hopeless case. Men, like women, come in all shapes and sizes. Whatever your size, there are a dozen someones out there who would not be taken aback by your front. But though men have been heard to say, "Extra pounds don't bother me. I'll just love you twice as much," slender sirens do have an advantage. One portly man I computer-dated (his computer profile had shrewdly displayed him from the neck up) told me how happy he was to see that I wasn't overweight. That really annoyed me. "How," I asked "can you have the nerve to want a thin women when you're so fat yourself?" He gulped and said, "I'll diet." I doubted it, and I didn't hang around to find out.

For those who do, there's a handsome dividend. Every study that comes out -- and more are coming out every week -- tells us that if you want to increase your chances of living a life that's both long and healthy, eat less and exercise more. I love to eat. When I come home from tennis or a long walk, I want to eat everything in sight. But self-controlling, I can look better, wear smaller sizes, and feel good about myself. I happen to have found my man already, but if I didn't, all of the above would help him find me.

Dieting isn't fun. You're engaged in a struggle with yourself all day long. And occasional uncontrollable eating orgy relapses are not unknown. But should a relapse occur, don't wallow in guilt and remorse. That could lead directly to the Tom and Jerry Response -- sitting at your kitchen table in your nightie, spooning relentlessly into a half-gallon of Rocky Road, loving every mouthful but hating yourself. Before you open that freezer door, stop and emphatically tell yourself that Rocky Road is a dead end. And remind yourself, too, that it's all up to you. Be a flower. Not a weed.

Let the prospect of gaining 180 pounds of new friend and lover help motivate you to lose 20 (or more) pounds of you. And (closing sermon) remember this: Make a habit of taking comfort food snacks to bed at night, and in the morning all you'll find beside you is a bunch of crumbs.

WINNERS AND LOSERS

Weight-watching plans are wonderful
They get you right on track
Watch extra pounds all melt away
Then watch them all come back.

Rx No. 5:
Love your body. It's the only one you've got.

Body image is a problem for a lot of women. Many of us had great figures once. Full-length mirrors were our best friends. But that was then, this is now, and our mirrors no longer tell us, "You are the fairest of them all."

Every woman can't be a size 6. And you might not want to be. But if your body is solid, which will happen if you enroll in and patiently follow a fitness program, you can feel like a 120-pound starlet and, in the half-light maybe even look like one, too. Easy to say, but for many of us not so easy to achieve. Says Fran plaintively, "I've put on so much weight the last few years, I feel huge. If I ever go to bed with a man again – and I don't know if I ever will -- he's likely to say, 'Ugh!' not 'Umm!'" Not to worry. The years won't have been all that kind to him either. He could be pretty "Ugh!" himself.

There's a problem here. Too many women in their 50s – even their 40s – and beyond have stopped loving the way their bodies look. I have a single senior friend who's charming, smart, attractive, would love to have a man in her life, but has been reluctant to date. "What," I finally demanded, after trying fruitlessly to talk her into dating, "is your problem?"

Nan confessed at last. "My buns," she confided. "They used to be firm. They're the opposite of firm now. Like Jello?"

"You don't have a thing to worry about," I assured her. "First of all, if this great event ever takes place, the man is going to be so busy – and so grateful -- that he won't even notice. Secondly, he's probably going to have a Medicare card in his wallet. How perfect do you think his body will be? He'll have flaws of his own he'll try to hide from you. Maybe even wrinkled buns." Nan joined a computer dating service shortly thereafter, so I guess my kicking butt helped.

A reference to "flaws of his own" is not mere speculation. When widow Helen and widower Harry agreed that they'd known each other long enough as friends to want to know each other more intimately, the thing she couldn't get out of her mind during their preliminary candlelight dinner was how he'd react to a body that bore little resemblance to the one that took her to her honeymoon. Trembling, because it had been a long time since the last time, Helen and her sexy negligee hid under the covers. A few minutes later, Harry entered, looking nervous and wearing silk pajamas that covered him from ankle to Adam's apple. When, some time later, she began to unbutton his top, he pulled back.

"No, Helen," he said, "I'd rather leave it on." She persisted. He insisted. It was only after she explained that he would be much sexier with his top off that he broke down and admitted to an inherited family trait that caused his body to erupt in bumps and lumps. "Nobody's perfect," she said, smiling to herself. "It won't bother me." And it didn't.

This has to be more common than you might think. It happens enough so that those anonymous people who invent jokes are joking about it. Like the mixed signals one eager senior lover is said to have received as he slid between the percales beside his 50-something girlfriend for their First Big Moment. He lifted the sheet. She shrank back.

"Oh," he said, disappointed. "I get it. Look but don't touch."

"Oh, no," she said, kissing him ardently. "Touch but don't look."

If the years have driven you beyond pleasingly plump, you can do all kinds of things to make yourself lovingly lookable. Rx's No. 3 and 4 point you in the right direction. In the meantime, until you get to where you want to be, cherish the fact that at museums many men linger before the paintings of Peter Paul Rubens, ogling his plump but indisputably voluptuous models, a number of whom, I suspect, have cellulite. It's for much the same reason that restaurants have menus. There's something -- as there is someone -- for everyone.

Just ask Mel. I did. He is proof positive that you don't have to be a Hollywood starlet to get a man's undivided attention. When I first met Mel, he was as stiff and unsmiling as a Strategic Air Command general during the Cuban missile crisis. His wife had left him after a 21-year marriage and he was, he told me, "hungry for affection." He'd had a series of disappointing dates which led only to another series of disappointing dates. Then along came a woman who had never won a beauty contest, but who knew how to fill a hungry man's emotional plate. With someone to hug and be hugged by, ever-smiling Mel is now described by one and all as "a new man." I haven't met his new woman, but I'm sure she's smiling, too.

Some women have decided somewhere along the lifeline that, for whatever reasons (familial genes, emotional problems, a lifetime love affair with desserts, or an inescapable addiction to McEverythings) that they are never going to look like supermodels and to hell with it.

Should this description fit anyone you know, all is not necessarily lost. My friend Iris was married to a man who owned a (there is no way to put this delicately) porn shop. Some of George's best customers riffled happily through the pages of magazines featuring women weighing in at from 175 to 300 pounds, and bought them all. Such customers enjoy what is known crudely in the trade as a "fat fetish." That, said Iris, worked to the advantage of her somewhat buxom cousin, Selma, who weighed just under 300. Even her mother had given up on her marriage prospects, but then along came Herb: good-looking, normal weight, and a real catch. "He never gave me a second look," added Iris, "but he went for Selma as though she was Marilyn Monroe."

Is Selma the exception rather than the rule? Possibly, but the rule is, "There are always exceptions." And Edie is another one. She has severe arthritis and carries enough weight for two people, but she's bright, interesting, upbeat, never misplaces her cheerful smile, and confided recently, with a certain amount of forgivable pride, "I enjoy sex regularly."

NEW AGE

This clothing spray erases

All wrinkles one-two-three

Could it be engineered

To do a job on me?

"My boyfriend says I'm beautiful.
That's the nice thing about older men.
As they age, their eyes age, too."

-- Daphne

Rx No. 6:
Don't let your past spoil your future.

"We finally got to where we could afford to travel," Leah said with a sad shrug, "and now the person I planned to travel with isn't here anymore." A baseball injury can in no way be compared to the death of a spouse, but there's a kind of guidance in what outfielder Mike Cameron said ruefully after a violent collision with another player. The accident left him with a concussion, a bloodshot eye, painful braces and screws in his mouth, and in need of surgery to repair his nose and cheekbones. But, said Cameron, "The worst has already happened. It's only going to get better from here." In fact, it did.

You've got a choice. You can spend the rest of your life sad, miserable, and mourning what you've lost, or you can dry your tears, cherish your memories and accept that your husband was wonderful, but he's gone and, God willing, you still have a lot of life to live. There's someone special out there waiting for you. Find him.

Her husband's final Alzheimer years were difficult for Leah. When she thought he was asleep upstairs, he suddenly appeared downstairs stark naked, which wouldn't have been a problem, except that her church women's club was meeting there. Early one Sunday morning while she slept, he took the car and, apparently driving on automatic pilot, headed it for Florida, stopping only when the car ran out of gas south of Washington. When she put him in a nursing home, he kept slipping out, taking a taxi home. So her husband's death had been, in a way, a relief and a blessing for Leah.

But thoughts like those felt like a betrayal of the man she'd loved for so many years. She wasn't about to follow the example of royal wives in India who centuries ago had gone up in smoke with their husbands on funeral pyres. But emptying his drawers and closet had been painful, and it wasn't until the last suit had been given away that she finally realized what her next task was: to find another traveling companion.

Not so Marie. "It's no use looking," she told sympathetic friends mournfully when her husband of 32 years died. "I'll never find another man like Joe. Anyway, I can't even imagine myself in bed with another man." She closed the door to fix-ups and stubbornly resisted exhortations from her sister and others that Joe would want her to find another partner, that she had many good years ahead of her, and that a man in her life would make them even better. Now, ten years later, a lonely and depressed Marie wishes she'd listened earlier. And hopes it's not too late.

Sheila's in a different part of the same boat. When her husband died suddenly ten years ago -- healthy one day, sick the next, and dead three months later -- it was a half-dozen years before she began dating again. But not often. Her specs were as detailed as an engineering drawing for a space station. He had to love dancing – with her as his star. He had to be tall (she is), not too old, with a good sense of humor, educated, and, above all, healthy. And, oh yes, she hated men who shaved their heads. With all her other requirements, Sheila's was the Impossible Dream, blocking her forward progress like the Great Wall of China. And so, except for the occasional fix-up, Sheila is still walking alone. (Don't!)

Part Two
CAPTIVATE

"Your energy will attract what you want."
--Gloria Vanderbilt

Rx No. 7:
Men are needy. Make the most of it.

I could say stupid, too. But that sounds a bit harsh. (Even if I said it in parentheses.) Certainly not all men. (I'm sure your father was brilliant.) And not in everything. But in relationships, they have a lot to learn. Take, for example, the widely respected former CEO of General Electric. If he's so smart, how come Jack Welch's divorce settlement with his discarded wife, Jane, cost him tens, possibly hundreds (attorneys sealed the figures) of millions of dollars?

The last time I announced that men are stupid was at a dating workshop in Connecticut in a room crowded with successful well-dressed men and women. I was prepared for objections from the males in the audience. Instead a man in back jumped to his feet. "You're absolutely right!" he declared. He was applauded.

It's almost universally true. Men go out in the rain without umbrellas. They misplace their keys and accuse you of moving them when you straightened up. They're suckers for flattery. They love to hear you say, "Oh, You're really interesting. I just love talking to you!" Or even (living dangerously), "You look like a very sexy man." It gets their attention. And they respond. (Well sure, we love flattery, too. But we know when a compliment rings true and when it's as hollow as an old oak tree.)

Men are needy, too. And not only in their need for affection. There's so much we can tell them that they need us to tell them. Like volunteering to help them shop (a great way to make points) and overcoming their genetic color-blindness by pointing out, "That's black, not blue," when they're about to buy slacks that don't match their jacket. They need us to remind them when they need a haircut, or when their nose foliage needs trimming. They're too macho and impatient to apply sun block. Then they wonder how they acquired all those hyena-like "liver spots," or, far more serious, incipient melanomas. They think making love is great, but watching NFL football is greater. ("Wait a darned minute, Honey. My team's on the five-yard line.")

Another thing. Mature men often have immature values. No matter how they look themselves, their search ads say they want *you* to be "attractive." And they have the nerve to specify "shapely" or "sexy." Every now and then I conduct an informal poll of unattached men of my acquaintance who have passed the half-century mark. They may be built like walruses, but they seem to believe that 40-year-old ex-super-models are their god-given right. I doubt that God thinks so. And when they unbutton their pajama shirts in the morning and inspect themselves in the mirror, I suspect that they don't either. They need help, and we can give it to them. Altogether now. Let's toss them a rope, and yank them down off Cloud Nine.

Hey, after a certain age, only a lucky few of us have great bodies. But before we take up the pursuit of woman-man happiness, we can make ours a lot better in the gym (bonus: exercise stimulates both the mind and the libido), and at the kitchen table, where portion control and self-control are ironclad and ice-cream and calorie-clad desserts are only once-in-a-whiles.

Plus, we can accentuate the positive. In that first get-acquainted phone conversation, we can be cheerful, positive, and enthusiastic. Also interested. Starting with, "Tell me about yourself." Humor helps, too. Like, "I may be a little plump, but I'm lots of fun." (Guys like fun in any form.) Phone flattery can make points, too. Like, "Your telephone voice sounds wonderful. Do you sing, too?") He'll probably deny it, but that'll move the conversation to interesting nostalgia – like the way his public school chorus teacher told him, "Mouth the words, but for heaven's sake don't sing them."

Have a good time, and then – as, of course, you will – make yourself as alluring as you can for that first date. Men want "attractive?" Okay, catch them with that. Surprise them with your brains later.

Rx No. 8:
Never walk your dog in a tattered T-shirt.

A dog can be woman's best friend if her neighbor's widowed brother happens to be visiting. So when you walk Rover, dress to impress. Every day. A delicious 20-year-old can throw on a faded stretched-out T-shirt for walking the dog and charm the tail off a squirrel. But when you're going on multiple times that age, you just look homeless, so don't be startled if men toss coins at you instead of hungry looks.

Don't dress your age. Dress your best. Wear cheerful colors, not dull drab browns that murmur meekly, "Please don't look at me." Consider contact lenses. Or, just as good and less trouble, a sexy fashion frame. It's all part of getting an edge. Granny glasses give you a granny look and that does not bring out the Rhett Butler in a man. Or the George Clooney for that matter. Accentuate your positives. Captivate with demurely daring cleavage. Men like "attractive?" So be it. What are you saving your best clothes for? They'll be out of style before you wear them. You've got 'em? Use 'em. If you don't got 'em, get 'em.

Get a friend whose fashion flair you admire to review your closet. Prevail on her to take you shopping, preferably when a good sale is on, and acquire a wardrobe that brings out the best in you. (If your children inherit $1,000 less, so what? Who earned it?) Then make space in your closet by giving away the rest to Good Will. Dress and do careful makeup even if you're going to be home alone all day. It's good for your self-esteem. Sure, it's tempting to save on laundry by wearing that nondescript sweat suit around the house. But you never know when some good-looking bachelor who's running for the town council will ring your doorbell. And even if no one comes, every time you pass a mirror, you'll like what you see instead of wincing and turning away, and you'll feel good instead of depressed.

Mona felt devastated on a Sunday morning when the man she'd dated twice happened to drop in to the store where she was buying paint she planned to use that day to give her apartment a new look. Things had looked good. He was interested in her and she in him. But now, instead of fully coiffed and made up, she was dressed for painting in loose pants and an old shirt, her hair was a mess, and her face was bare of make-up. Some men, less shallow, might have understood. This one didn't. End of phone calls. End of story and the possible happy ending.

No matter what the occasion -- supermarket shopping, picking up the dry-cleaning, a walk in the park -- don't look frumpy, look alive. Picture yourself applying for a job, with every date an interview. To sum up: The one look you don't want, whether walking to the mailbox or walking the dog, is looking like something the cat dragged in.

PASSING FANCY

Does she know she's wearing her breakfast
That egg stain on the front of her shirt?
Why tell her? She'd just be embarrassed.
(But what she doesn't know could hurt.)

Rx No. 9:
Smile, smile, smile.

Personality has ever been a plus. You're at a wedding. A couple is dancing nearby. You wonder, "How did that Plain Joan attract that Handsome Harry?" Could it be her bank account? Well, maybe. But more likely, it's the way her smile illuminates the room, shedding light, optimism, and happiness wherever she goes. (Yes, smiles do that. Especially if they've been whitened.)

Marie is such a woman. Buxom, with average looks, she says, "I've always had men come on to me." Her secret -- and it can be yours -- is, "I'm very friendly. I'm not afraid to start conversations. Men don't like needy women. I radiate self-confidence. And I smile at everyone." A smile is like a rose blooming in the desert. Driving by, you may not notice the desert, but the rose will definitely get your attention.

Why do we love babies? Their sunshine smiles make up for what's in their diapers. Why do we love dogs? Their smile is an enthusiastic welcoming wag of their tails. A smile warms like sun breaking through clouds on a stormy day. It's a universal language that says, "You please me." It hints at joy and pleasure to come. Why, it's even more infectious than a yawn.

You, not outside forces, are in charge of your state of mind. Smiling, studies show, is nature's Prozac. So what's a good way to elevate your mood when you're low? Bend the corners of your mouth up into a smile, instantly messaging your brain, "Get happy! Get optimistic!" Your brain flicks a switch and, lo and behold, you forget your troubles and, to your amazement, suddenly feel wonderful. Most of the time. I asked a workshop group, "What's the most important piece of advice to give a single woman over 50?" A 65-year-old woman who had recently changed from Ms. to Mrs. gave this succinct reply: "Smile at every man you meet."

Her answer brought a smile to the face of every woman in the room. Including mine.

Rx No. 10:
Persist. Persist. Persist.

Shining Star, run by a charming Tibetan journalist, is a popular diner on Amsterdam Ave. on Manhattan's Upper West Side, and Paula is – or was -- our favorite Sunday brunch waitress. I have never collected stamps. I've never collected coins. If I have a hobby, it is trying to make sad people happy. Paula, though very attractive, was grimly unsmiling when she brought us our usual brunch frittata. She lived alone and was, not surprisingly, lonely. She was in her late 30s (somewhat younger than women we're writing about, but in a situation familiar to many), felt life was passing her by, that she'd never find a husband, and, said mournfully, "I'd like to have children before I get too old."

I gave her my usual lecture: "Persist, persist, persist. Respond to every halfway decent man on whatever internet dating service you join." "I've joined two of them," she said. "I went on a few dates, but I never met anyone I liked or, I guess, liked me. I've been doing it for a long time, and I'm fed up. I'm quitting," she added vehemently.

I got upset. "You mustn't quit," I said. "You're a very special woman. Don't ever give up. Promise me you'll keep trying. It's the only way to make something happen." She smiled. "Okay. Okay. I promise."

A dozen or so Sundays later, we sat down in our regular booth, divided up the newspaper, and waited for Paula to finish up at a nearby table. She hurried to us, leaned forward, and kissed me on the cheek. "I met The One," she said happily. "He's kind, considerate, fun, responsible -- and he loves me. And I love him. And it's all because you forced me to persist."

Well, if you're not persisting, you're resisting. Paula didn't, and now, I'm happy to report, she's married and in love with a wonderful guy.

Rx No. 11:
You get no second chance to make a first impression.

Marilyn is ready. She wants to meet a man. She's on a couple of e-date services and things are progressing. But when I tell her that the man of her daydreams could be just around the corner in cyberspace and she needs to seize any opportunities that present themselves, she is doubtful.

One of her problems is knowing how to build a conversational bridge and cross it comfortably. I gave her some simple but useful examples: "Where did you get that beautiful tie? You have excellent taste." Or, "I love your moustache. It gives you such pizazz." Or, "What an interesting watch! May I see it up close?" A man will take that as either a compliment or a ploy. A ploy is a compliment, too, so either way he's going to be pleased. The worst he can say is, "Excuse me, I'm late for an appointment." And don't take that personally, because maybe he is.

Marilyn and I were at a restaurant together when a good-looking silver-haired man sat down at the next table, accompanied only by a book. "Marilyn," I said, "here's an opportunity. Seize it." Marilyn recoiled. "You mean start a conversation with him? Just like that? What if he snubs me?"

"Okay, Marilyn," I said. "Watch what happens." I observed the man as the waiter brought his dinner. Then I leaned toward him. "Gee," I said, "that's a lot of food. You're so slim. How can you possibly eat that way and not get fat? I'd love to know your secret." He smiled. "It's more than I usually eat," he replied. "I worked up a major appetite at the gym." I introduced Marilyn, who then got into the conversation. He gave us his card. I don't know how this will turn out for Marilyn, but she got the idea. Namely: if his looks appeal to you, any appropriately-aged single man who passes within ten feet of you is an opportunity. Seize it.

Seize it, too, if you happen to be in a bus or a train and an interesting looking man happens to sit in the empty seat beside you. If you just stare ahead or out the window, absolutely nothing will happen except breathing. But if you remind yourself that words are bridges, you could erect a virtual Golden Gate Bridge before you get to your stop. The words can be situational. Like, "Is that an Army bracelet you're wearing? Where did you serve?" Or, "I love your suit!" Or, "That's such an interesting ring. Is it from college, or from pitching a no-hitter in the World Series?" They may lead somewhere. They may lead nowhere. But, as they say about the lottery, "You never know."

At a party, this being a unisex world, you might say, "I came alone and I don't know many people here. I love this song. Could we dance it together?" But if you say, "Isn't this a wonderful party?" and he says, "Yes," and walks away, don't be crestfallen. No big deal. We all get rejected now and then. And maybe he just had to go to the john. Look around, target another Alone Ranger, and try try again.

Part Three
COMMUNICATE

"I'm going to Europe with my aunt. I love her dearly, but I wish I were going with a man I loved instead."
--Louise

Rx No. 12:
Make friends with a computer

Mildred is an unhappy widow. She dropped in on me one day with a shopping bag in each hand.

"What have you got there?" I asked.

"Pocketbooks," she said. "I went shopping. Tell me which one you like best."

"Hold on, Millie," I said. "You've got a million pocketbooks already."

"I know," she admitted, "but the only thing that makes me happy is shopping."

Mildred is wasting her days malling. She should be volunteering at a local hospital or mentoring at a local school. And she should be shopping for a man on a good dating website.

Doreen is. "I felt like a teenager starting all over again," she said enthusiastically, "except that when I was a teen, computers were just science-fiction. Oh, I mess up sometimes, but once you get the hang of it, computer dating is almost as easy as making a cup of coffee. And it beats waiting for my phone to ring."

There's a high greater than caffeine in sitting down at your computer, punching in your password, and reviewing the half-dozen new faces (roughly meeting your specifications) that have miraculously appeared overnight. You'll probably reject most of them, but there are always "could-this-be-the one?" possibilities. It's a daily something- to-look-forward-to that injects an electrical charge of anything-can-happen excitement into your life. And if it doesn't, so what? Tomorrow is another day.

Of course, the very idea of shooting your face and bio into cyberspace in the hope that Mr. Reasonably Wonderful will spot it and call can be worrisome. It can even feel, well, embarrassing. ("Oh, did you see Ellen's profile on findyoursoulmate.com? She must really be desperate.") That's what you think catty friends might say. But, first of all, they'll be scanning for men, not women, so they won't even know you're there. But more important, as the philosopher-statesman Seneca is reputed to have said, "What others say about me is none of my business."

The computer is a miracle matchmaker, but if the idea of dealing with yet another complex electronic device freaks you out, you're not alone. Fortunately, helping hands abound. Many local libraries, schools, and senior organizations offer free or inexpensive classes. Private lessons at reasonable prices can be found in most weekly neighborhood classifieds. Best of all, a platter of chocolate chip cookies should buy you enough time from a computer-savvy young neighbor, niece, or grandchild (they're all computer-savvier than we are) to teach you all you need to know to get "wired" and registered for computer dating.

About those chocolate chip cookies. Don't eat too many.

COMPUTER LITERACY

When soft or hardware baffles me
And chaos is resultant
I have a simple remedy
My eight-year-old consultant.

Rx No. 13:
Maintain a high computer profile

Like author Norman Mailer, you'll be writing "Advertisements for Myself" on your computer. And the more they allure, the better you'll fare. You'll need to post a profile and a couple of your most flattering recent photos (your wedding picture's gorgeous, but it's a tad out of date) chosen to stop traffic and get his attention before he hits the cursor and moves on to the next contestant.

The profile is a brief autobiography, and as one on-line male put it colorfully, it resembles a woman's skirt: short enough to be interesting, but long enough to cover the subject. It's a good idea to sew that skirt when your mood is positive and energized. Then show it to a couple of friends -- including, if possible, a male friend -- whom you can trust to critique it honestly and constructively.

Profile dishonesty is the worst policy. It's not a felony to subtract two or three years from your age. Almost everybody does. (When you meet and 'fess up, he'll likely do the same.) But beyond that -- relationships are built on trust --fib no more. Yes, you'll get lots of hits and even dates when your ad brags, "fabulous figure." But if your hips don't measure up to your hype, don't expect second dates. Elizabeth learned that to her sorrow. Her web profile, describing her as a "tall, brainy, drop-dead beautiful blonde," won her more hits than Mickey Mantle. Lots of first dates, too. But – untruth in advertising will do it every time – no seconds.

Similarly, you can write all the romantic catch phrases in the world ("ready to fall in love again" or "one-man woman looking for the right man"), but the right man won't find you if your picture is a carelessly chosen snapshot squinting into the sun that makes you look forlorn instead of fabulous. One study has shown that profiles-with-photos get ten times as many hits as those without them. Bottom line: A professional photo op emphasizing your best features, taken in the afternoon after a morning session with a good hair stylist is a worthwhile investment that will greatly improve the odds. It may cost a few dollars, but in matters of the heart, it doesn't pay to be half-hearted.

Rx No. 14:
Play the cyberspace numbers game.

Computer dating is a lot like a raffle. The more tickets you buy, the better your chances of winning. So don't register with just one e-dating service, sign up with two or three: Match.com, eHarmony. com, JDate.com – all of which have "mid-life" or "senior" age listings. Or google and scout sites specifically embracing the 50-Plus category.

Not immediately, of course. Sign with only one at a time until you're comfortable with the process. But don't put all your eggs in one skillet. E-mail a daily dozen of appealing gents. Many won't respond, but – do the math -- all you need is one. If, like my friend Amy, you complain, "No one answers my e-mails!" the answer is, "Try changing your message. Try changing your picture. Or, to put more arrows in Cupid's quiver, get on more dating services."

That worked for Amy, but not immediately. You have to be patient, determined, and, even when things aren't going your way, appreciate the adventure. Why not? It's a long time since you felt as though you were starring in a Kate Hudson dating flick. But don't think of each date as a potential husband. Relax and enjoy the ride. Savor the moment.

And don't forget good old-fashioned pre-computer newspaper personals, return calls to which usually cost a few dollars, but can be a great source of possible suitors. Inserting your own personal won't cost all that much either. A good ad could keep you busy answering the phone and dating forever and a day. If there's a phone number for you to call and you have to leave a message -- which is the way classified personals work – make sure your tone isn't flat and monotonous. Barbara panicked and hung up. "I'm going to call back, but what do I say?" she wailed. "Say, 'I'm exactly what you're looking for. I'm fun. I'm sexy. I'm smart.' And say it with enthusiasm" is what I told her.

I could advise that course with enthusiasm of my own because I'd already taken it successfully in answering an ad in the New York Times. (Yes, personals are "old- fashioned," but a lot of people still use them.) The advertiser wanted someone "well-traveled, short, thin, and attractive." I phoned and left a message, "I'm exactly what you're looking for." He called right back, but unfortunately wasn't what I was looking for. He was a rancher and wore the Stetson of the cowboy trade. Very romantic, but my memory of a friend who took a trip to a Colorado dude ranch and had a horse fall on her, shattering her hip, was still fresh in my mind and did not help his cause. Still, I should have given him a chance. Even a second or third. It takes that long to make a fully informed decision.

Beware of rogues and scoundrels. Take sensible precautions. Never give a man your phone number until you've phoned him first to get a sense of what he's like. (Of course, that will only work if your phone is equipped to hide your personal ID.) Don't reveal personal information. And (you knew this already), don't invite him to pick you up. (You won't have your father there, looking grim, to inspect him.) Arrange to meet in a public place -- a Starbuck's, a diner, a museum. If he insists on meeting at your place on a first date, put him on your "To-Don't List." There are Computer Casanovas out there -- both male and female. Your chances of encountering one are slim, but knowledge about them is power.

You've read plenty about the females of the species: sexy young -- or comparatively young -- wenches who marry older men, inherit their estates when they die prematurely, squander their money before the family can file for their fair share, and then move on to the next victim. Male gold-diggers, worming their way into hearts and beds, operate pretty much the same way.

Sandra's experience warned her that she needed to spend more time on the phone asking searching questions before agreeing to meet a computer date. He'd sounded nice enough, offering to meet her at an excellent restaurant – which sounded better than the usual, "Let's meet for coffee." But when she arrived, he said, "Oh, my goodness. It closes for lunch. But look – there's a McDonald's down the street."

Sandra ordered a fish sandwich and French fries. Saying he'd had a late breakfast, he ordered a Coke, but then hungrily proceeded to make her fries disappear in a pool of ketchup. Between morsels, he launched into a lecture on how sex was good for the complexion and circulation, and, by the way, there's a nice motel near here and we could have a terrific afternoon improving our complexions.

She refused him politely and said goodbye forever, thinking as she got behind the wheel of her car that he probably would have used her credit card to pay for the motel.

Okay, let's sum up. As you check out the newest arrivals on your computer screen, think of yourself as a fisherman standing on the banks of a stream. It's teeming with trout. You can just stand there holding your rod and reel and catch nothing, or you can cast again and again until you've landed a prize-winner. Final message: remember, if you're not satisfied with what you catch, you can always throw it back, and try try again.

Shirley Friedenthal and Howard Eisenberg

MATCHMAKER, MATCHMAKER

Dates and marriages
Used to be arranged.
Then along came the internet
Hmm, things sure have changed.

Rx No. 15:
Age is only a noun.

It's also a label, and labels can fool you. I've met 75-year-olds so fit and frisky they could pass for 60. Some look so young they get "carded." My friend Arthur popped into our computer skills class recently with a smile on his face wide enough to bridge the Mississippi. (Well, almost.)

"Why so happy this morning?"

"I just got a haircut."

"I can see that. And it's a good one. But it's something to celebrate?"

"Absolutely. It was Senior Monday and the barber charged me the regular price."

"That's a good thing?"

"It was a great thing. He didn't think I was a senior."

A healthy older man who walks and works out regularly can be a better OO (One and Only) than a younger man who takes every drug known to his pharmacist. A man is, after all, only as old as the contents of his medicine chest. Many women adamantly refuse to date "older men," because, "it could lead to a relationship, and I don't want to end up as a nurse to some sick old man."

The thing is there's no predicting which partner will be the one needing care and which the caretaker. But even if the new man in your life filled it with joy and companionship for only three years, they'd be wonderful years which, focusing on his "number" and failing to seize the moment, you'd have missed.

Anyway, how many times have you wished you had a man around the house who could help you figure out how to work the camera on your new digital phone? Or carry your groceries. Or, best of all, provide male companionship and affection. Someone you can talk to and laugh or cry with. So judge that internet advertiser on what he says and –when you meet him – not on his age but how he's aged. Anything else risks locking out the man of your dreams whose only flaw is a wrong number.

FORGET ME NOT

You forgot that movie's title?
Not to worry. Nought to fear.
You've only got a problem when
A senior moment lasts all year.

Rx No. 16:
Consider a modern (but big bucks) matchmaker.

Dating services are strictly an if-you-can-afford-it short cut option, but they can be an important investment in finding the right friend, lover, husband, or all-three-in-one. After my husband died, I clipped an ad for a service that guaranteed me 18 quality pre-screened dates in 18 months. The catch was the cost. I thought it over. $5,000 was a lot of money. On the other hand, this was about the rest of my life. Meeting that many "carefully screened and selected men" might be worth mortgaging the farm.

In fact, one at a time, the service pretty much delivered them to my door. One was a successful entrepreneur, another an IBM executive, a third a pediatrician, the fourth a retired businessman who shared my enthusiasm for tennis and was an excellent player. I had 14 more to go and looked forward to every one of them as an adventure in dating. But, ironically, I had registered with a far less costly computer dating service as well and that's when I met Howard, leaving the other 14 (representing, if I did the math correctly, an unused balance of $4,648) still out there dating other women. Oh, well. Good luck to them.

But choose your dating service carefully, or you'll need not just good luck, but a good lawyer as well. My friend Alma, impressed by her first meeting with a very slick matchmaker, signed on the dotted line. She was promised a minimum of a dozen dates, but it was more than a month before she got the first one, and he never called back. From another woman he'd dated, she found out why. He had an interesting ambition. He wasn't a two-timer, he was a one-timer. He wanted lots of dates with lots of women, but, for some odd reason – only one from each.

The months went by -- eight or nine of them with no dates -- and Alma, ordinarily a reasonable woman, grew increasingly angry. Every time she called the service, she was told, "We'll find you someone wonderful. Just be patient." After a half-dozen calls, Alma made a different call -- to an attorney. She went to court and won, only to learn that her matchmaker, apparently not without experience in such matters, had not a single accessible asset in her own name. Alma is still out some $5,000, but her lawyer is confident that, one way or another, she'll get her money back. (Meanwhile her legal fees continue to mount.)

When and if it's your money, do some homework before you sign the check. At a minimum, check with the Better Business Bureau. And ask for references from previous clients. Not just any references. The names and phone numbers of women whose dates led to one of two places: either a long-term relationship or a stroll down the aisle. If you decide to go with a matchmaking service, don't be unreasonable. It's not a good idea to propose a list of desired qualities resembling the add-ons on a pizza order. And make sure the service has a number of eligible males signed up in your geographic area. A service offers matches, not miracles.

GOOD HEAVENS

It's tough to find the perfect partner
So let us pray.
If nothing else works
That may.

Rx No. 17:
Spin like a spider

Yes (I've said it before and I just might say it again), dating is a numbers game. If a hungry spider quit after spinning a single strand, it would catch no flies. Nothing but the breeze. To catch a man (I know that sounds unseemly, but would trap, lure, or seduce sound better?) you've got to spin a web. You've got to network. To go where the men are. To e-mail anyone who sounds interesting. To keep your options open.

You've begun a promising e-mail chat with NATUREBOY8. When he says he loves hiking, you say, "Au revoir." Not so fast. Try it. First of all, walking's great for your health. You might learn to love it and him. Or, alternately, he might be so happy smooching on your couch that he turns into your personal potato. So say yes to a date, and see what happens. (You didn't like it. Or him? You got too sweaty? Take a good hot shower and wash that man right out of your hair.)

When I was "looking," an interesting but pragmatic pediatrician's e-mail to me said, "You sound wonderful, but you're two hours away, and with my schedule it just wouldn't work." He was probably right, so I let it go, but I ought to have said something we should say often when we want relationships to work: "I'll meet you halfway."

So never say never. What does Eileen want out of the rest of her life now that her long-ailing husband is gone? She wants to dance. So the phone rings, it's that new e-date acquaintance whose profile sounded so interesting that she gave him her phone number. Eileen says, "I'd love to go dancing!" He replies: "I'm afraid you're ten years too late. I used to be a runner. I used to love dancing. Now I've got arthritis and I walk with a cane." Eileen blurts out, "I don't think this can work" and says goodnight.

Not good. Snap judgment. You have to go out with a man at least two or three times to find out if he could be your OO. (I'd better retranslate that: One and Only.) The woman who expects perfection is going to spend the rest of her life alone. And maybe water aerobics could help his arthritis.

Valerie met a man at an Early Bird restaurant dinner in Florida while visiting her sister, shrewdly choosing an empty seat next to him at the counter instead of sitting at a table alone. She struck up a conversation ("Would you please pass the salt and pepper?" got it off to a good start), found him interesting, and dated him several times. He visited her in Boston for a week and then went home. "I liked him," she told me. "He called and said he misses me. But he lives too far away. What's the point? I'm not going to see him anymore."

"Val," I said, "Florida's not a two-day drive anymore. It's barely three hours by plane. You say you like him. You enjoy him. And he misses you. By the way, how was the sex?" She smiled. "Fantastic," she said. "Well?" I asked.

Valerie's going to Florida to see him again, only this time she's staying longer. They'll be exchanging visits until who knows? Maybe she'll move to Florida. Maybe he'll move to Massachusetts.

Some men are rigid as an iron bar. But if they appeal to you anyway, try adjusting to them as, in the end, they must to you. There'll be men who don't want to go to restaurants, who want to go to bed early, who, worried about tomorrow, are conserving dollars today. In time, you might reform them. If not, you have to consider saying (unlike Leila who limits herself by refusing to date a man who won't pick up the check), "If you're on a budget, let's just go Dutch."

The rules have changed since women dated in organdy. If you can afford it and he can't, pay for your half of the cruise. Among other things, it sends a message (something his children may be worried about) that you're not after his money.

Rx No. 18:
If you don't ring the bell, you don't make the sale.

That was true for old-time door-to-door salesmen, and if you wait passively for your doorbell and your phone to ring, it could be true for you as well. Use personal ads, computer matches, networking. Be aggressive. Have a plan. Think of it as shopping for a man. If you don't see what you like at one store, try another. There are dozens of men out there who would love your company, but how will they get to hold your hand if it's in your pants-suit pocket? You've got to pick yourself up and shop instead of being one of the too many who just sit and wait for something to happen while life and male affection pass them by.

If you're at a singles dance, don't wait for an invitation. Men, too, can be shy, and your chances of meeting someone are a lot better if you're a creeping vine than if you're a wallpaper wallflower. Walk up to an interesting looking man and, with a big smile, say hello. Introduce yourself and, with another smile, surprise him with four little words: "Are you here alone?" Or (with a role reversal smile), "I'd love to dance with you. How about it?" The first time it might be hard to get these words out, but what's the worst case scenario? He says no, but he's flattered, and you snatch victory from the molars of defeat by asking, "Well, do you have a single friend who's as cute as you?" Maybe he does.

You may not want to go to a singles dance alone, and there's nothing wrong with going with friends. But once you get there, for heaven's sake, don't all cling together like long-stemmed roses in a vase. Separate and stay separated. Men dread walking up to a fortress of women busily engaged in conversation and then have to break in to ask the one they've spotted from afar for a dance. It's embarrassing for them, and it's doubly embarrassing for the women who aren't chosen. Very often the man's too intimidated to make the move, and a lose-lose situation ensues for one and all.

Entire books have been written on the subject of "pick-up lines." Mostly they're for men. But we've got the vote and a lot of other equal rights, and you won't go to jail for approaching a man who appeals to you, cell phone in hand, and saying, "I just bought this and I've been looking for someone who looks smart to help me figure it out." Okay, it's the old dumb blonde approach, but gentlemen have always loved heroically changing tires for helpless ladies on the thruway. Complex multi-tasking cell phones are not only the modern equivalent, you don't have to be dumb to be baffled by them.

Honesty could be the best pick-up policy of all. Like, "I've been racking my brain trying to think of a good reason to talk to you because, well, you look really interesting. I couldn't think of anything that wasn't totally embarrassing. But how about it? Let's talk." That kind of candor can be very refreshing. Plus, it's flattering. And who knows? Maybe he's been racking his brains about you.

Most important, be the lioness ever ready to pounce whenever an interesting quarry comes along. Like the woman who got lucky when her car was unexpectedly hit from behind by another motorist. She got out of her car. He got out of his. She took one look at the well-dressed pleasant-looking man approaching her, and instead of barking, "Why don't you look where you're going?" said sweetly, "It doesn't look so bad. Let's just exchange licenses and phone numbers. Gosh, it's such a little dent it may not be worth fixing." They began to date with the first phone call.

Don't wait for Opportunity to ring your bell. She who is vigilant will find it everywhere. Thelma, recently widowed and unhappily alone, opened her newspaper one morning to find a photo and story about a surgeon whose marriage proposal she had refused 35 years earlier. Impulsively, she phoned him. The doctor was so happy to hear her voice that he couldn't wait to see her, cancelled his plans, and they had dinner the same night. But not all stories have happy endings. (Well, you knew that.) Their dinner was bitter-sweet. He would, said the doctor, happily propose all over again except for one thing. His wife was chronically ill. He just didn't feel he could abandon her. Thelma understood and moved on. She reads her newspaper very carefully.

Nan bravely converted defeat into victory when she found she'd written down the wrong address for a matchmaker's meet-and-greet cocktail party. After anxiously checking half-a-dozen adjacent buildings and coming up empty, she took a deep breath and stepping into a nearby coffee shop, announced loudly, "Excuse me, but I've got the wrong address for Sybil Gordon of Dates & Mates? Does anybody know where I can find her place?"

Most diners shrugged or didn't even look up from their plates. Nan was about to exit sadly when a gentleman sitting alone at a booth stood up, smiled pleasantly, and said, "I don't know Sybil Gordon, but I'd love it if you'd have a cup of coffee with me." Nan did, abandoned her search for Dates & Mates and has been seeing him regularly ever since. "He's so nice," she says. "Maybe this will be the one."

(Late bulletin: He wasn't, but she learned a valuable lesson: that you get better results speaking up than piping down.)

Like Nan's, your motto should be, "Nothing ventured, no one gained." That's been Iris' motto for years, and her success with tossing demureness to the wind and replacing it with practically naked aggression could fill a memoir. Like the time, working in a bank near closing time, she barked to the other tellers, "Close up! I just saw the man I'm going to marry." He was one of the last three customers and her strategy steered him to her window. She read the address on his deposit slip and, looking up, smiled, "My, we're neighbors!"

"Not really," he said, when Iris told him her address, "but you live a couple of blocks from my brother. I go there often to play chess."

"Really," said Iris, carefully spinning another strand around the man on the other side of the partition, "I always wanted to learn to play chess."

"I could teach you," he replied, and the romance was off and running -- straight, three months later, to the altar.

NAKED TRUTH

**Your phone hasn't rung
For many an hour?
It will just as soon
As you step in the shower.**

Rx No. 19:
Go where the guys go.

Legendary bank robber Willie Sutton, whose name will be remembered when most U.S. vice-presidents are forgotten, was successful (until he was caught) going (he famously said) where the money was. If you want to get caught, you might consider joining a boat club. That may sound outlandish, but it worked for a clever California woman I met. "Men," she thought, "love boats. If I go where the boats are, that's where I'll find the men." She joined a sailing club. Men, she found, were delighted to take her sailing and show her which side was port and which starboard. One of them proposed that she become his First Mate and she accepted.

History Associations attract more men than women. Dabble in politics at local political club meetings. Try bridge clubs or bird-watching. Hiking or walking clubs are another good place to meet a man. Even if you don't get a guy, you'll get fit. Or join a gym, where more and more older men are trying to stay in -- or get into -- shape. But first acquire a flattering workout outfit. Admire their muscles (the ones who don't have rings on third finger left hand), and ask their advice: "How do you adjust the weights on this shoulder press machine?" You could follow that with, "Are you doing anything after your workout? How about a cup of coffee?"

You could end up losing some weight and gaining both a guy and bone density. And maybe this scenario is a long shot, but older men in the gym love proving they're still in prime time. When an interesting acquaintance tears his meniscus overdoing 50 pounds too many on the leg press, offering "to be there for you at your surgery" might be going a bit unrealistic, but your empathy and sympathy could earn a campaign point or two.

Find people who like things you do. Church and synagogue over-40 singles groups are both safe and – occasionally – successful. If it's a supper, maneuver demurely into a seat beside someone who's caught your eye. Seating between two men – a small miracle not beyond the realm of possibility – doubles your chances.

A dating machine that seems to be catching on – though certainly not yet everywhere – is the "Invitation Only Private Party," which works this way: You buy a membership from the hostess arranging the parties. You contribute the names and addresses of three reasonably desirable bachelors. Other women do as well. The hostess sends invitations to the single men whose names she's collected and runs the party – cocktails, canapés, the works – which can open opportunities, if not flood-gates.

When opportunity knocks, open that door. Fast. Toni saw the name of an old beau in her community college catalog. She had dated him 25 years earlier between marriages, and now she signed up for the course he was teaching. He recognized her immediately, and was happy to take up where they'd left off. They're now "going steady." You may not know the instructor, but you can certainly get to know him by hanging around to ask a question after class. (Especially if you made sure the instructor was a "he" when you registered.)

When you take courses at community colleges or elsewhere, select those that are likely to be of interest to men. Like Civil War, Islam, politics. Choose courses with care. You're not going to meet a lot of men in a History of Feminism class, but you might in Painting, History, or Chinese Cooking – which is, by the way, where my daughter met her husband. Some men love to cook (unfortunately, it often shows) and think how much easier your life will be if you should happen to connect with one.

Bachelors have to eat and a good place to meet them is the supermarket. The one buying a single steak is a likely target, and an easy way to strike up a conversation is to ask if he knows where the walnuts are. Or, for that matter, the dishwasher detergent. Ellen doesn't ask. She bumps. After identifying a likely target, she casually crashes her cart into his while innocently examining the tomato sauce shelf. A conversation can then ensue ("Oops, I'm sorry. Oh, let me give you my drivers' license number. And would you like my phone number, too?") and, if they like what they see, a date may ensue as well.

As with all ice-breakers, if your quarry answers icily and turns away, don't take it personally. Maybe he's just gotten an audit letter from the IRS. Forget him and, undiscouraged, explore elsewhere. Like (Warning: joke coming up!) the woman who entered an elevator, locked eyes with a handsome fellow passenger, and said, "You look like my third husband!"

"You've had three husbands?" he asked, surprised.

She smiled coyly. "Oh, no," she replied. "So far only two."

Now there's an icebreaker.

Shirley Friedenthal and Howard Eisenberg

MAKING CHANGE

I love movie stars and leading men

My love will never falter

Until I guess the day that I'm

Invited to the altar.

"Your car won't start?
Try turning on the ignition."

-- Eddie Fisher

Rx No. 20:
Network as if you were NBC.

Networking ignites. Carol, volunteering at a library, shyly asked a fellow volunteer if she knew any available single men. To Carol's delight she not only did, but offered to introduce her to them. Networking. It's good stuff – the same thing advertisers do when they want to tell the world about their products. You're not going to reach 20 million people, but all you need is one.

Shrinking violets bloom unseen. So turn off your Shy Button and start spreading the word that you're available, and keep spreading it. Tell just about everyone you know or meet that if they know any nice appropriately-aged men, you'd love to meet them. Ask your hair-dresser. Ask your children. Ask the postwoman. If you live in a high-rise, ask your elevator man.

That's what I said: your elevator man. Ellen's friendliness and her generous holiday tips to her building's elevator operator had him taking her seriously when she told him she was "looking" and asked if he knew any single men in the building around her age who might be doing the same. The blood might have drained out of her mother's face had she heard her ask the question, but this was fearless modern networking at its best, and he helped her make a successful connection.

Vivian, a recent divorcee, approached me some years ago at our bridge club and said, "I hear your husband was a doctor. I'd love to marry a doctor. You must have lots of doctor friends. Could you fix me up?" I didn't, but she continued to network boldly between hands until she was "fixed up" with the unattached brother of one of our members. They've been married for five years, and it wouldn't have happened if she'd been too embarrassed to ask. You never know when Cupid will choose you for target practice, but it helps if you supply the little fella with some extra arrows.

Edith did just that when her favorite uncle was dying of cancer in Texas. Every time she phoned him, her uncle's buddy, taking care of him to the end, picked up the phone. Their conversations gradually lengthened, moving beyond her uncle's condition to his past and hers. After Edith's uncle died, his friend paid her a visit and, eventually, became more than just a friend.

Life -- a new life -- can sneak up on you after a mate dies. Suzette a French tour guide, told us how her 72-year-old grandmother brought flowers to her late husband's grave every Wednesday morning. After a while, she noticed a pleasant-looking gentleman doing the same at his wife's stone. They talked. They liked what they saw and heard. With their deceased spouses as matchmakers, they became a couple.

Said Suzette, "My grandmother's late husband had been so strait-laced and frugal that if she wanted to go dancing, she climbed out the window after he fell asleep. She and her new man bought a car together and traveled, doing all the things she'd been denied. They kept separate homes, visiting each other on alternate weekends. My grandmother always had something to look forward to. 'My,' she'd say, 'it's Wednesday. How nice. In just two days, I'll be going to Pierre's house."

In South Florida, where women outnumber men the way the Persians did the Greeks at the Battle of Thermopylae, some women unembarrassedly take matters into their own hands. They print cards with their e-mail addresses and phone numbers and boldly offer them to men they chance to meet. Is this brassy and brazen? Not if it works.

Sometimes women find their new man at a bereavement group, and, of course, that's equally true of men -- like the man who lost his wife and, for the first time, went to a group that met for lunch in the back of a restaurant. When he arrived, he asked the manager where the group met. "You're going in there?" asked the manager. "You're going to have a great time." He went in and found that he was the only man with 17 women. Six months later, he married one of them.

My friend Shirley, whom I've known for more decades than I care to count, wasn't sure about joining the hospital's bereavement group when Irving, her husband of 40 years, died of cancer.

"I pictured a bunch of women listening to each other's stories and soaking packs of tissues," Shirley recalls, "and I wasn't sure I could take it. Actually, there was some crying, but it was all about sharing feelings, and I could see right away that letting it out was going to be good for us. There were more women than men, of course. One of the men interested me – he was very articulate -- but I got the impression he was attracted to another woman. When she talked about going on a cruise to start life over, he asked,'Hmm, would you like company?' Truthfully? That annoyed me."

As Shirley left the final session, the man who'd asked that annoying question fell in beside her. "Jerry," Shirley said as they walked toward the elevator, "you're a very attractive man, and it's time to move on. There's a woman I'd like you to meet."

Jerry stopped and took her hand. "Shirley," he asked, "how about speaking for yourself?"

"I lost interest when you asked Carol if she'd like company on her cruise."

"You can't be serious. I was just kidding around!"

By the time the elevator arrived, they had agreed to dinner. By dessert, both knew that a new relationship had begun.

Part Four
DATE

Rx No. 21:
Go it alone.

"There's a Golden Oldies dance at church tomorrow night," one of your friends says. "Priscilla and Rose are going. Let's go with them. It should be fun." Pause. "We might even meet someone." Not a bad idea. You know that the only meeting that's going to take place if you sit home reading this month's book club choice will be between your your couch and your butt.

It's worth a shot, but when the music starts (I've said this before but it's definitely worth repeating), much as you like your friends, you don't want to be standing around alternately small-talking and looking glum as one-quarter of a bouquet of wallflowers. That, then, is the moment to separate from your chums and take a solo stroll -- enabling a man too intimidated to approach a formidable foursome to attack a less daunting target: the lone maiden.

I speak from experience. You'd be amazed at how much dancing I was able to enjoy – except when I picked a man with two right feet – simply by cruising solo. And, call me brassy or call me practical, I didn't always wait to be asked. If an interesting man hove into my horizon, I never hesitated to strike up a conversation by simply complimenting him on his tie, his haircut, or even his blinding Hawaiian sport shirt.

Lone-wolfing need not be confined to dances. Fran, dressed to the eights (the nines would have been a bit over the top) and feeling a bit self-conscious about buying a ticket-for-one, nevertheless went solo to a week-night concert. At intermission, a man who'd been sitting in the row behind her moved to an empty seat beside her.

"Are you a regular?" he asked, and after a conversation about favorite performers, took her out for coffee-and afterward. The next week – and for many weeks since --they've attended together. Will their relationship become permanent? Will music-lover become lover? Stay tuned. It's too soon to know. But, in the meantime, she's enjoying male companionship and friendship, and one thing's for sure: if she'd attended that original concert with girlfriends, the person now in the seat beside her would be – right -- a girlfriend.

LOOKING FOR MR. GOODGUY

It takes persistence. Perseverance.
Faith. Hope. Pessimism restrained.
Plus, of course, a dating web site
Nothing ventured, no one gained.

Rx No. 22:
If at first you don't succeed, it's his fault.

You are almost certain, if you do much dating, to meet a Dr. Charlie. Charlie married his high school sweetheart and he was a one-woman man until, inevitably, dissolving their togetherness, death did them part. Charlie loved his wife, but subscribed to Playboy, and he's had a secret seven-year itch for 37 years. Now he plans to scratch it one woman at a time for as long as the supply and his libido lasts.

Well, that's fine for Charlie, but he's going to leave scores of women in his wake wondering what they said or didn't say, did or didn't do, that turned him off. ("Was I too shy or too aggressive? Underdressed or overdressed? Should I have invited him to a home-cooked meal?") Nonsense. Tell yourself you ran into a Dr. Charlie, mentally push him off a cliff, and go on to the next one.

Some men will reject you. You'll reject some men. See each date as a learning experience. Keep improving. Quitting is not an option. Above all, don't let a date that goes sour depress you. No date should be considered make-or-break. Rather it should be looked forward to and enjoyed as an adventure – even if it ends unhappily. For example, you e-mail back and forth. He makes a date and asks for another picture. You send it. He cancels the date. Or, this happened to one woman I know, he rings your doorbell, takes one look, says he just remembered another appointment, and leaves. That could be extremely depressing, but don't let it get you down. Far better to shrug it off and think like a baseball player: I struck out today. I'll hit a home-run tomorrow. And, hey, it's not me. It's him. (Or, if you can think grammatically when you're upset, "It's not I. It's he.")

That's what I told Inga when, close to tears, she reported that a man she'd dated a half-dozen times had casually informed her that he'd been simultaneously seeing another woman for several years. "What should I do?" she asked frantically." I really like him. I felt a strong attraction to him from the first day we met. He was a dream come true, and now I find he was just toying with me. I don't want to be half a harem."

"Calm down," I said, "and think about the situation. "If you can't live with it, give him an ultimatum and a deadline. Tell him he has to decide on which of you he really wants. That he definitely can't have both. On the other hand, if you can live with it, play a waiting game. Be patient. See what happens. You enjoy his company? You like going out with him? Be loving. Be understanding. Get a great new hairdo and some sexy new clothes. And by being even better than your usual wonderful self, help him make up his mind that you're the one he can't live without."

When Mike died, I was on the other side of Inga's situation. Well, not exactly, but similarly. I met a college professor who, after three dates, phoned me one evening and got my answering machine. Next morning he called again. "Where," he demanded, "were you when I called last night?" I had been, I told him truthfully, out on a date. "Shirley," he declared indignantly, "I refuse to go out with a woman who's dating other men." I was far from ready for that kind of commitment to him, and was immediately certain after his ultimatum that I never would be. "I won't go out with a man who dictates the rules," I said, and dropped him like a hot pot handle. It was no great loss. He was as overweight as he was pompous.

Jean could use some botoxing, but says "No way!" to it. She carries 30 pounds more than the dress window mannequins that we're supposed to resemble. But she doesn't let that drag down her supreme self-confidence that if she loses one man, she can find three more. She'd moved into a brand-new high-rise building when she discovered that the incinerator room was directly across the corridor and tenants in a hurry had piled foul-smelling garbage outside its door. Jean picked up her building phone and dialed the concierge.

"I started to yell at him," she recalls. 'Where's your staff? What kind of building is this?' But the man on the other end kept trying to interrupt to tell me it wasn't his fault. That just got me angrier -- until I realized the phone lines had crossed and I was denouncing a fellow tenant. But he was a good sport. He told me he'd just thrown a holiday party and since I hadn't come, he'd love for me to come enjoy some of the leftover food and drink.

"I did and we became first friends and then lovers. That is until he surprised me with the news that he had a long-time date to go skiing in Switzerland with his ex-girlfriend. I told him that if he did that, by the time he came back I'd have a new man in my life. When he returned two weeks later, I did – a man three floors up who had very romantically kissed me (with my blessings) when I walked under the mistletoe at our building's entrance. That one I married."

So select, don't settle. In my huntress period, I dated a brilliant dentist who seemed to know everything about everything. One thing he didn't know was when to stop eating. He was, in fact, a walking encyclopedia with a paunch. "I don't like bellies," I said, pointing at his. (I could never work for the State Department.) "Not to worry," he replied, "I'll go on a diet." In fact, as he took me to the best restaurants (yes, he was rich, too), he did seem to be cutting back -- a bit. The first time he drove me home, he leaned over and gave me a peck on the cheek. The second time he located my lips. The third time he opened his mouth so wide, I was afraid I'd fall in. It was goodbye Arthur, and on with the plan to select, not settle.

The fault may not always be his. The quickest way to disable a first date and guarantee there'll be no second is to wear perfume as though it's an article of clothing. Sure, the glossy advertisements assure you it's seductive. And you just happen to own a bottle of Chanel No. 5 that your late husband gave you for Valentine's Day 30 years ago, and, well, doesn't it improve with age? Whoa! To some men it's an aphrodisiac (which can make the first date a hit and run affair), but to others it's an invitation to asthma. If you're planning to wear it, first ask if your date is allergic to perfume. Otherwise, your date may end five minutes after it begins.

You can't judge a book by its title ("Gone With The Wind" could have been about a hurricane) or a man by your first date. A perfectly good man could seem down and depressed because he's had a bad beard day. If you think you see someone special beneath those dark clouds, give him a second date, and a third. Maybe, if he's improving, even a fourth. After that, having found that his black clouds are a permanent wave, it's time to look elsewhere.

Active dates (picnics, hikes, art museum visits) can be better than passive ones (coffee, brunch, movies). They give you shared experiences. It rains on your picnic and you forgot to bring umbrellas. You both love flaming sunsets. It turns out you both love Renoirs. There's more to talk about. You're more relaxed. It's about you and the activity, not about salmon medium-rare.

If the first date goes splendidly, wonderful, and on to the second. If it's more like a train wreck, put it behind you. Forget it. It's time to board another train.

ASSIGNING BLAME

**One catastrophic date
Shouldn't bring you to a halt
Just tell yourself this truth:
"It was his fault!"**

Rx No. 23:
He doesn't have to be Richard Gere (though that would be nice.)

Okay, so he's not Hollywood-handsome. If he's endearing enough, even if he has two right feet, you can still waltz happily through life together. So go out with anyone who sounds marginally okay. And (it's worth repeating, so I shall), unless he turns you off faster than a light switch, consider dating him three times before you dismiss him. As you may remember from chapter two, it wasn't until the fourth date that I was sure Howard was the guy for me. You just never know.

Age and looks should both be irrelevant in deciding whether you like or don't like a man. I made up my mind to be an equal opportunity dater -- to give every date at least a couple of encores. (A basketball belly occasionally changed my mind.)

Bonnie would love to hook up with a Harrison Ford, but she's a realist and pretty darned sure that a rugged Handsome Harry would not have eyes for her. "At my age," she shrugs, "you have to take what you can get. Fred isn't exactly the Dream Boat I wanted when I was 20, but he's only 25 pounds overweight, which nowadays is practically slim, and we have some good times together. I love opera and he doesn't. So big deal. He stays home and watches the Lakers while I'm out watching "Madame Butterfly." But when I come home, I'm not alone."

Different strokes for different blokes. A friend told me about a man in a village in Vermont who mourned his wife upon her death, but after a decent interval sat down and made a list of every single woman in town, 50 and above. One by one, he invited all six of them to a home-cooked dinner. One by one, he invited them to marry him. One by one, they refused. I've no idea what was wrong with him. Maybe he was a terrible cook. Maybe he had toxic bad breath. Maybe they'd heard he beat his wife. It's hard to believe that not one among his candidates was willing to take a chance on love. Or, at least, on a couple more dates before making up her mind that he was hopeless.

Eve has a mental picture of her ideal man. He is, she tells me, tall, good-looking, physically fit, and a good dancer. But a picture in your head isn't as good as a good man in your bed. What Eve needs to do is tear up that picture and take men as they come. Date them, get to know them, and perhaps discover that a short man who trips over his feet instead of the light fantastic has so many wonderful other qualities that, eureka, the 8 x 10 glossy of Fred Astaire (you know – the dapper guy who danced in those great old films) in her head is replaced by his.

Bonding with a new man takes time and, most of the time, several dates, at least. Again, it's like gluing two sheets of paper together. It takes four corners and a blob in the middle. Every experience together is another blob. When you've done enough, your bonding is complete. Or not.

Another thing. It's not fair to compare. Harry's gone. It'd be great if he could be cloned, but that's not going to happen -- anyway not in your lifetime. So don't keep searchng for Harry. Look for a new love for a new chapter in the book of your life. And welcome an Imperfect 8 with open arms. At a certain age, the Perfect 10s are gone. Sure you'd prefer a Lexis, but a Prius can give you a darned good ride. And don't forget the power of a woman to change a man. Not the first day, but over time. So, two pieces of advice: (1) Don't demand perfection -- even if you're perfect; and (2) Give him a makeover after you land him. If he needs it.

MY DREAM GIRL

You should be beautiful and thin
And when we argue let me win
You should be radiant as May
Love to travel. Pay own way.

You should be sexy. Just for me.
When I watch football let me be
At restaurants say, "Let's go Dutch!"
Hmm, could I be asking too much?

**"The only thing worse than sleeping
alone is eating alone."
--Tovah Feldshuh in
"Love Came Lately"**

Rx No. 24:
Raise your tolerance threshold.

So what if he bangs the toilet seat and doesn't cut his nose hairs until they look like the Amazon rainforest. Bite your tongue and hold your horses. Don't make a big deal out of little things. Improve them when you can call him yours. In the meantime, be an Equal Opportunity Dater with lukewarm first impressions no deterrent and multiple dates – unless he has LOSER written on his chest in capital letters – your rule. Love at first sight is rare when you're 35 or 40 years out of your teens and, "He's not my type," is broad-jumping to conclusions you could regret when your dance card is empty next Saturday night. Moss may not grow on you, but sometimes a man will.

Martha and Sidney hit it off big time in their first few phone conversations. Things got even better when they met at a local restaurant for dinner, and Martha told her friends, "I think this is it." One more date and she was sure. But then she invited him home and her dog greeted Sidney with open paws – at which point he backed out the door and, through a paroxysm of coughs, said, "Sorry, Martha. I'm going to have to go. I'm allergic to dogs."

So what does a girl do when she has to choose between a man and her dog? Martha chose Fido and she's been sorry ever since. She's thinking now that what she could do is give the dog to an animal-loving friend who lives nearby, retain visitation rights, have her apartment cleaned professionally, and then get back on the phone with Sidney. If it's not too late.

Don't be turned off at first sight if a man looks like a tramp in sneakers and jeans on your first date. There may be a pearl in that rough shell, and, if you decide that's so, you can take him shopping later. A little subtlety helps. Start by taking him to the Men's Department to buy him a shirt for the birthday you missed because you hadn't met him yet. Women are born with a gene for style, but since it's missing in most men, they need a woman to say, "Take it. It's perfect!" Men may not be color-blind, but most don't know black from navy, and how to combine colors is an Agatha Christie mystery to them. They haven't a clue how silly they look in shorts when they wear their socks pulled up high instead of folded down. We save them from having to rely on the sometimes biased opinions of store staffers (if one can be found), and they love us for it.

He's overweight and that bothers you? If it does, you might say, "I'm going to save you some money starting right now, and add ten years to your life. Let's share our main course for dinner." If you like him, but not the way he opens his mouth when he kisses, tell him it turns you off, not on, "so how about trying a different technique?" But after three dates, if you're bored or your reclamation project seems hopeless, terminate and move on.

Vera didn't. She hated being alone after her husband died. When she met Fred, bells did not ring when they kissed, and conversation flowed like ice in winter. But he seemed to like her and she no longer found herself alone and reading a book while waiting for the waiter at restaurants. Vera decided that they had enough in common so that when he proposed she could willingly say yes. They married, and she's been sorry ever since. She doesn't confide that to friends, but it's easy to see that she's bored, that she'd be better off with a book, and that they're strangers in a loveless marriage.

Interests in common may be good, but sometimes – because they add new dimensions and spark to your life and relationships – uncommon interests can be better. Rhonda and Marshal would never have been introduced by a matchmaker. He loves hiking and skiing. She prefers the Great Indoors. "But when we met," says Rhonda, "we clicked immediately. And I don't have to break a leg skiing to get his attention. By mutual agreement, when he goes on a skiing trip, I go traveling with my friends."

So, "he's better than nothing" is not a smart choice. Neither is, "He's way too different from me." If you're certain that's the way you feel, it's time to move on. Hey, you got one. You can get more.

MY DREAM GUY

I'd love to make love to George Clooney
Robert Redford would not be half bad
And I wouldn't mind if DeCaprio
Confessed he was our love child's dad.

I could even go for Tom Cruise
If he'd stop preaching weird Scientology
I'll just search 'til the chemistry's right
Then lie back and enjoy the biology.

Rx No. 25:
Dealing with the guy who's shy.

Some men are just plain shy -- like Ed, whom I met one afternoon at the library while picking up the book club book I'd reserved. He told me he'd been divorced three years and added, not very enthusiastically, that he'd been dating another woman for the past year. "Stop me if I'm wrong," I said, "but you don't sound very excited about her. What's missing? Is she affectionate?"

"She kisses me goodnight. On the cheek."

"Have you tried for more?"

"Well, no. But she is good company."

"Wouldn't you like more than that?"

"Well, sure. But she doesn't seem interested."

"Don't you talk about it? Have you ever mentioned it?"

"Uh, well no."

One wholly impersonal year. I couldn't believe it. So I gave him the Shirley lecture: "You're a good-looking intelligent man. You're hungry for affection and you're not getting it. You need someone you can hug, someone who'll hug you back. But you need to say what you need, not wait until it's offered. Women can be shy, too. Especially older women who didn't grow up with 'Sex in the City.' Sure, you can live without affection and intimacy, but life is a whole lot richer with it."

I guess he was listening. I went back to the library several weeks later to return the book, and there was Ed. "You look different," I said. "You're smiling. Did you meet someone new?"

"Yes," he said, his smile widening. "At a party. I drove her home, and when she invited me in, that seemed like she liked me, so I kissed her. I guess I was right, because she responded. A lot." He smiled again. "I'm seeing her again this weekend."

His cell phone rang. The librarian glared. He took the call outside, and then returned enthusiastically.

"That was your new friend, wasn't it? What did she say?"

"She can't wait for Saturday night."

The woman who didn't respond will be going out with the girls.

It works both ways. My friend Sally connected with Neil on the internet. Two dates later, she reported, "He's nice, but he's dead from the neck up. Maybe from the waist down, too. We had good times both times, but he didn't so much as give me a peck on the cheek goodnight. I'll go out with him again, but only so I can meet his friends. Who knows? I might like one."

"Not so fast," I said. He's probably just shy. Maybe got slapped on his first date at 14. Permanently traumatized. Why not try being what used to be called 'a little forward?' Now it's just plain honest. Ask him why he didn't kiss you. Say kissing is one of your favorite sports. Then see what happens. I guarantee a lot will."

Reaching out is the name of the game -- from the first time you meet to the first time you date. Even if it's only for a movie. "Okay," says you'll go out with him, and that's an okay reply. But "I'd love to!" says you're as interested in him as you are in the film.

Lorraine is charming and attractive but somehow never married and, until Harry, an accountant, came along, hadn't had a date in 15 years. Harry, she said, was a nice guy and they dated three times. On the last date, she rewarded him with a quick good night peck on the cheek. He hasn't called since.

"You're too stiff," I told her. "That peck on the cheek was like baiting a mousetrap with catnip, and it's definitely no way to catch Harry. Or Tom or Dick for that matter. If he's sitting on the opposite side of the room, invite him to join you on the couch. When the time is ripe, give him a hug. Let him know you're interested. Don't just brush lips when you kiss, plant them. There are a lot of shy men in this world, and if the messages aren't there to read, they'll go home with their tails between their legs thinking that they're failures, that they're not good enough for you."

On Louise's second date with Mark, she invited him to the Metropolitan Opera, where she had season tickets. Afterwards she invited him for a drink in her apartment in a nearby Lincoln Center high-rise. If ever a man received an engraved invitation to be, well, naughty, it was that night and it was Mark. But Louise was too embarrassed to make the first move, and he was too shy. The moment passed, the evening ended, and they never saw one another again.

There's nothing like touch to bridge a gap, so reach out and – as Louise did not -- touch someone. You're on a date and something he says registers with you. You feel like squeezing his hand, but you hesitate, thinking, "That would be too aggressive," and you smother the impulse.

Wrong! It's going to feel good to you and send a message to him. Men, even mature men, can be shy or afraid to make a move for fear of rejection. Let him know he's got nothing to fear. It's something he'll take away from the evening, and it'll help win you a return engagement.

So will cheerful follow-up phone calls. If you like someone and he fails to call, don't just sit there twiddling, call him. Not plaintive. Not accusatory. Senior men (who may go through periods of loneliness and depression) like and benefit from upbeat and cheery. Call not once, but, if necessary, twice: "I really enjoyed your company. I'd love to see you again." It's an ego-booster and they love it. And it's a message that even the shyest guy can understand.

James was a retired Pepsico executive, apparently more accustomed to commanding men than women. He was good-looking, dressed well, had some hair, and (by now you know big bellies are a major no-no for me) no paunch. But date after date – six of them -- he escorted me to my door and, as politely as a State Department intern, said goodnight. It was, I felt, time to take charge.

"Why don't you ever kiss me goodnight?" I asked. "Are you afraid I'll bite you? I won't. And I won't slap you either." He looked surprised but pleased. "Oh," he said, "I didn't think you'd want me to." I put his mind at ease. "Not so," I said. "Let's try it." And he did. Very nicely.

CASUAL ENCOUNTER OF THE WORST KIND

Our glances lock
And then they break
Perhaps you think
I'm on the make.
The fact is that I'm rather shy
I smile. You smile.
But we pass by.
If only your brown eyes had signaled:
"Approach me with impunity."
But you and the moment are gone
Another lost opportunity.

Rx No. 26:
Put on your Oprah hat.

So your first date gets underway, and he is eerily quiet. He runs his fingers through what's left of his hair. He jingles coins in his pocket. He studies the menu as though it's on the law school entrance exam he's taking tomorrow morning. Well, some men are talkers and others need to be uncorked. But the last thing you want is to sit at a restaurant table in silence. The CD they're playing in the background might as well be a funeral march.

Kissing is a universal form of communication, but we can't spend all our time lips-to-lips, and anyway it's much too soon for that. What to talk about? Certainly not the weather – unless it's snowing in July. Or pouring cats and dinosaurs. Imagine you're Oprah and start an interview. No politics – things could get unpleasant if he's Red and you're Blue, so, for the time being, stay Pastel. You need to find out about this man, to find the corkscrew that will open him up. One thing's for sure. Saying tearfully, "You remind me of my late husband," is guaranteed to close more conversations than it opens.

Women can always find something to talk about, but, as one man told me, "We pretend to be strong and silent, but the truth is we don't have all that much to say. Our goal all our lives was to work, to provide for our families. Some of us are pretty boring." This is, of course, not true of all men. And, with questions about his past life, a woman can reawaken half-forgotten memories that he'll enjoy recalling and reciting.

"Were you big on dancing when you were young?" Pam asked. "Then -- but not now," Vernon insisted, pointing out that it had been more than 30 years since his last foxtrot. "It's like riding a bike," Pam encouraged him. "You never forget." She had asked the right question. With gentle prodding, he responded. And, Pamela says proudly, "You should see him cut a rug now." (Pam's got a long memory. When's the last time you heard that expression?)

Ask lots of questions about his life -- from his childhood on up to his divorce or the loss of his wife. Most men enjoy talking about themselves, and they love a rapt audience. (Well, I guess we do, too.) They appreciate people who care enough to be interested in them, to want to know what makes them special. If you ask the right questions, no man is boring. There's a best-selling memoir waiting to be opened in each of us. So take his off the shelf. Open it up and you'll make a friend, maybe a guy friend, for life.

Catherine hit the jackpot when she asked her date, "What's your favorite college memory?" After a moment's thought he reeled off story after story of his semester in Mexico. Getting picked up by police with three buddies for smoking pot and diplomatically avoiding jail. ("This is not a bribe, senor. It is a fine.") Of the lovely senorita he and a friend met on a bus with her duenna. The chaperone quickly became part of a double date. Of hiking in Guatemala jungles. He was euphoric with nostalgia in no time and told Catherine, "I haven't thought about that in 100 years. Thanks for asking."

So play "Life Story." Ask him about favorite high school and college memories, military memories ("Were you part of The Greatest Generation?"), family and work memories ("What's the one thing you remember best about your mother? What was your father like?"), favorite teachers and sports, firsts like the first time he played Spin the Bottle, his first date, his first car, his first job. Turn that into a game by relating your firsts. And get him talking about himself by priming the pump, as any good interviewer does, with little confessions of your own. ("I was terrible at sports. They always picked me last.") In all things, stay upbeat. Don't talk about your arthritis unless he talks about his. And when you've asked your questions, listen to the answers – with eye contact so he knows you're really interested.

Find out what his interests are. Yours may be closer to his than you think. Sometimes they're distant – like he's a Boston Red Sox fan and you can't tell a baseball from a matzoh ball. It's not a criminal act to check the sports pages in season so you can jump-start the evening's conversation with the latest injury report. Or, better yet, go on the Red Sox web site, find out when they're going to play your home team, and surprise him with a pair of tickets – one, of course, for you. That's guaranteed to make him almost as much a "you" fan as he is a Sox fan.

I'm not saying there's something fatally wrong with lulls in conversation. Silently squeezing his hand, for example, speaks volumes. But that, with luck, will come later.

Rx No. 27: Help him with his baggage.

Still grieving for his wife? Divorce embittered him? Constantly worried about his job or his business? Uncomfortable because it's a long time since he was out with a woman? His mother, who wants to keep him to herself, warned him to beware of gold-diggers? Nobody's perfect. Be a good listener. Be a good conversationalist. Make him so happy that, in time, he checks his baggage at the door.

Rx No. 28:
Make much of touch.

Reach out and touch someone when the vibes feel right. Like him? Embolden him! Men can be wary of making the first move out of fear of rejection. Reach across the table, place your hand over his and say, "This has been such a wonderful dinner. Thank you." There's magic in touch. So be touchy. Squeezing his arm brands you a scarlet woman? Maybe 100 years ago, but not today. Slipping your hand in his just says, "I'm yours." (Or could be.)

I'm not saying that all men are weak and subject to manipulation. They're more like puppies. They love to be stroked and they come back for more. Their egos need stroking, too. They crave attention -- especially from women – and affection makes them purr like, well, kittens. They're needy, so give them what they need. And that can include cuddling on a sofa – which can feel so good that he won't even notice that it didn't go all the way. (Well, maybe.)

I've saved – and am reluctantly revealing – the best for last. I hesitate to suggest it because you just might suspect that I'm a brazen hussy. (Then again, maybe I am.) But you know what? Sex may be a concealed weapon, but using it this way is not a criminal offense.

Anyway, here's how it works. You can give your shy but loveable date a major hint about your feelings if, as you stroll arm and arm, you squeeze his forearm so that his elbow presses against your bosom. You, of course, pretend that you don't realize it. He pretends he doesn't notice it. But you'll both enjoy it, and he'll instantly recognize it as a semaphore signal that reads, "You're Number One on my Hit Parade."

MAMA KNOWS BEST

My mother used to tell me
"Darling, always look your best.
And always wear clean undies."
Well, I guess you know the rest.

Car accidents don't worry me
But I share Mom's quaint obsession
And when I meet my Mr. Right
I'm sure to make a great impression.

Rx No. 29:
Make every date great.

What you do will have a lot to do with *how* you do on a date, so don't just wait for the doorbell to ring. Think about ways to make your dates different. Women are better planners than men. So spend some time planning. Don't make it a movie. Unless he's a groper, the evening will end with your knowing not much more about him – and he about you – than when it began.

More imaginative ideas will put an appreciative grin on his face. You live in New York? Suggest lunch in Philadelphia topped off by a visit to the amazing Barnes art collection. (Spending 90 minutes on the road each way – or, more ecologically correctly, on a train -- affords a great chance to get to know one another.) Consider a hike with a picnic built in along the way. (A double date can be twice the fun, and it allows you to park a car at each end, so you can drive back instead of walking it.) If hiking has as much charm for you as a flu shot, drop it and just do the picnic.

Unless his allergies are a problem, he'll love a picnic. Have you enjoyed one lately? Probably not. Picnicking takes us all – including him -- back to our childhoods. To burgers and hotdogs on the grill (before we knew they weren't particularly good for us), to Mom's delicious home-made coleslaw, and to the lemonade that was Dad's specialty, but you helped squeeze the lemons. (Of course, today you'll want to cut the sugar bowl calories in half.) A basket of fried chicken (easy on the deliciously fattening skin) is sure to recreate another happy memory.

A wide-brimmed hat could be fetching (if you look good in wide-brimmed hats), and you'll need sunglasses and sun block. He probably won't remember the block, and you can show how valuable a helpmate you'd make as you gently (and dare I say sensually?) spread it on his exposed body parts, hinting at romantic moments to come.

But for a first or any other date, nothing beats, "Let's go dancing!" If the only place you can find has a cover charge or a minimum, you could show you care about the wear and tear on his wallet by offering to split it. That's a test. He'll probably say, "Don't worry. I'll take care of it." If he doesn't, well, you learned something about him.

Dancing's the best legal way ever invented to get close to a man and remind him how sweet and yielding a woman's body can be – even one that's a tad overweight. If you're enveloped in that wonderful old Big Band sound, so much the better. He'll feel warmly nostalgic when he hears the Beatles oldies. They'll remind him of wonderful teen days gone by. (They weren't all that wonderful. His date may have resisted when he tried to kiss her goodnight. But if you like him enough, you can erase that memory.)

Or be a sport. Watch a sport. He loves football? Okay, even if you think a quarterback is your change at the newsstand, make your date memorable – and an unexpected surprise for him -- by treating him to tickets for Sunday's game. He'll love showing how smart he is doing play-by-play commentary for you. And he'll owe you big time. If you dress warmly, this is one date that'll be a win-win feel-good experience. (If you don't, you won't feel anything but numb.)

So think of interesting things to do and places to go – with that occasional offer to pick up the tab. Not just brunch or dinner. Nature walks. Concerts. Bowling. Museums. Walking tours. Put your mind to it and you'll think of a dozen things to do. If they're things you'll enjoy, you'll have a good time even if the date chemistry is a fiasco. If, on the other hand, all goes well, it's a hint that life with you would never be boring.

When date is done, it's not a bad idea to pick up the phone next day to thank him for a wonderful time. It's more than good manners.

It's good strategy. No need to say, "I'd love to do it again some time soon." It's implied.

If you never hear from him again – which sometimes happens -- don't take it personally. Just cross him off the list and move on.

"**Where there is no hope, we must invent hope.**"
-- Albert Camus

Rx No. 30:
Don't endlessly seek the spouse you've lost.

Defying all logic, both widows and widowers do it. One bereaved husband spent three years searching for a clone of his wife, chronically depressed and with tears welling up in his eyes if a date happened to ask about her. His wife had been very special and they'd spent many wonderful years together. But he couldn't find her for a very simple reason: God doesn't make carbon copies.

When you go on a date with a photograph of your late spouse engraved in your heart, the date is as unlikely to succeed as ordering a rib steak in a vegetarian restaurant. My friend Alice has been alone for 17 years and she hasn't dated once. "I had such a good marriage," she said. "We were together since high school. There's no way I could find a husband as wonderful as Joe. I'd rather finish my life alone."

I asked a question. "Did you and Joe ever argue?" She paused for a moment. "Well, yes," she admitted. "We fought plenty. But making up was wonderful." Everybody fights. A marriage without disagreements would be boring, and, though I don't know any, I'll bet that even saints lose their tempers now and then. The point is that Alice has wasted 17 lonely years of her life, when, if she'd been open to it, she could have met someone as wonderful -- or almost as wonderful -- as Joe. I think she regrets it now. And, it's never too late.

Rx No. 31:
Don't take the pot off the stove before it boils.

Avoid the temptation to ask, "Do you love me?" Men hate that question. When they feel it, they'll say it without prompting. Before then, you're just asking them to lie. If you're a smoker going out with a non-smoker you'd like to know better, you need to announce that you're in a cessation program. And it better be true. Otherwise the cessation will include future dates.

We all want love to last longer than that. So avoid moves that could end it before it begins. During a lull in the conversation, don't pull pictures of nephews, nieces, or grandchildren out of your wallet. Don't speak ill of your first spouse. (Old bitterness, like old wine, does not travel well.) And don't instantly reject your date because he doesn't look like Harrison Ford. You'd rather hold out for tall, flat-bellied, and ruggedly handsome? Sorry. You're living in a celluloid world. Sean Connery is not registered with findyoursoulmate.com.

Rx No. 32:
Don't close your mind. Open your purse.

Judith was depressed. She was tired of living alone. She wanted a man in her life. Then she found one. "He's really nice," she said with a smile in her voice. "I finally got lucky." That was a month ago. Yesterday she was back to being depressed.

"It turns out that he doesn't have any money," she said. "He wanted to go Dutch to everything. I told him that's not the way it works. I want a man who's willing to pay all the bills."

"Hold on," I argued. "You drive a Lexis. That jewelry you wear didn't come from Walmart. You can afford to pay half. Or more. Last month you told me how much you liked him. Now you're chasing him away?"

With an attitude like Judy's, partners are hard to find. Thea's way works a lot better. She's in a ten-year relationship as happy as a lobster that escaped the pot. A half-dozen dates after she met Richard, he confessed one night that he was worried that the size of his 401K and other assets were not sufficient to keep her traveling and living high on the hog -- at least, no higher than its rump. Thea was not about to let a good man go because his bank account didn't match hers.

"It's no problem," Thea assured him. "We can go 50-50 for most things. You buy your show ticket, I buy mine. And on the big things, if necessary, we can make it 60-40. It's only money, and I've got more than I need."

Good for Thea, I say. Who wants to make love to a bank book?

Rx No. 33:
Go for his heart through his mouth.

Surprise him. Bake him a cake. Or go for the jugular – actually, the belly – by inviting him for dinner. Preferably but not necessarily home-cooked. Good take-out will do. But an excellent way to a man's heart is still through his mouth. In the Sun Belt, they tell 101 jokes about the Casserole Brigades that form as hopeful women parade to a new widower's condo with the dish each hopes will gain his attention and win his heart. But it's no joke. I know one lonely divorcee – and I'm sure there are many more – who followed that path into a successful relationship.

It helps if you're a good cook, of course. But the conversation is as important as the food. If it doesn't flow like the wine (bringing a chilled and appropriate bottle could set you apart from the pack), that's not a good sign. But try it. You have nothing to lose but a casserole. And if he's the kind of man you'd like to live with, he'll invite you in to share it.

Rx No. 34: Beware the married man who wants you to scratch his seven (or 14 or 21) -year itch

"Oh, come on," you say, "Who needs that advice? I wasn't born yesterday." You'd be surprised at how many savvy women, who should know better, do. Sophia, for instance. Her husband had been ill for many years. For the last three or four she'd been too busy taking care of him and running a small business to think about anything (or anyone) else. When he died, she realized how much she missed having a man in her life. A few months later, she began looking for one.

Sophia is 59 but looks ten years younger, and one date was all she needed to attract keen interest from a dentist who confessed on date number five that he was "married but miserable." Sophia greeted that piece of information with mixed emotions for the simple reason that they were in bed at the time. And, like Lady Chatterley, she hadn't had that fabulous an evening in a very long time.

Sophia gave the situation a lot of thought when the man who was actually somebody else's man left. He'd held her tight and assured her that she was the best thing that had happened to him in years. He'd said that now he was certain that he wanted a divorce. But three months and a dozen trysts later, he was no longer so sure. "For the time being," he apologized, "divorce is impossible. My wife is terribly depressed. She's on medication. She suspects something, and she's threatening to kill herself if I ever leave her. How can I walk out on her now?" But, the soul of generosity, he offered a thoughtful (some might say self-serving) alternative: "We can get together every other weekend." Sophia's initial response was unprintable. But a few days later she told me, "It's crazy, but I still love him."

Where have we heard that before? But you know what? If she lets go, she'll find someone else just as good or better – and single. (Late bulletin -- she has.)

Divorced men can be as good as any other. My son married much too young – at 22 – and it was a mistake from the moment he said, "I do." But a divorce, many dates, a relationship or two, and 20 years later, he found the right woman, and he and his wife (also divorced) couldn't be happier. But some divorced men carry a toxic torch – like handsome Philip, whom I dated a half-dozen times after my husband died.

Phil's alluring wife had left him suddenly, returning to her native Argentina to marry an old flame, leaving him with their two children. Phil was a romantic. He showered me with flowers, took me to fine restaurants, and, kissed me ardently under a Rodin sculpture at the Metropolitan Museum saying ardently, "I can't resist you. I had to do that." (I had a little trouble resisting myself.)

Phil was every woman's fantasy -- mine anyway. After years of caring for my husband during his final illness, I was eager for candlelight and flowers, but I felt that something was wrong. Between dates, I thought about Phil's frequent and bitter comments about his ex-wife. They disclosed, it seemed to me, a sharp and unremitting undercurrent of anger toward all womankind. It disturbed me so much that, despite his gallant wooing and physical appeal, I reluctantly decided to break off our relationship.

So don't let a divorce get in your way. We all make mistakes. But don't continue to date a time bomb who returns bitterly to the same subject: "My wife was a bitch." You could be the next one burned by the wrathful anti-feminine torch he's carrying.

Part Five
MATING

Rx No. 35:
Be friends before you're lovers.

Friendships that last are built on a foundation of compromise. You like tennis and he likes bowling. So what could be more obvious? Take lessons in each. You like to go to church Sunday. He'd rather watch "CBS Sunday Morning" and "Meet the Press." So agree to go every other Sunday, or find a pastor who's more interesting. He loves to walk. You think it's boring and you'd rather drive. Discover that when you're walking and talking, the miles fly by, the pounds fly off, and your heart grows stronger as well as fonder.

Fond though they may be, some women lose interest in sex earlier than others, almost as though the charge in their libido batteries is slowly fading out. Katrina, a trade journalist in her mid-50s, told me, "I used to have a 1000-watt libido. Now it's down to about 100. I'd sit in a meeting and fantasize about going to bed with every man at the table. Now I don't care about sex. What's more, I don't care that I don't care. All those women's magazines ignore the needs of older women. Their cover lines are for 30-somethings -- like 'How to Hype Your Sex Drive.' What we need is, 'Don't Worry When Your Sex Drive Dies.' My guy is more concerned about his libido slipping than I am. I'm happy with hugging, but I keep wondering how long he will be."

Faith couldn't care less. We sat under adjacent driers at Tony's Salon and when the subject turned to sex – which, I confess, not solely for literary research, it often does with me – she confided, "My boyfriend wants to sleep with me. I don't want that."

Renee is different. In her early 60s, she placed a personal classified ad in a weekly newspaper ending with, "No objection to sex." Boy, did she get answers! Really nice men, and, she confided, really good sex. Scandalous? Some would say so, but I say just plain honest. And in the end it led to a warm and mutually satisfactory relationship with a gentle humorous man in his 80s that's as much about love as it is about sex.

Sex is the ultimate connection between two people who like each other. Sometimes love precedes it. Sometimes it follows. Which comes first doesn't really matter. Something that does matter is HIV testing. Along with the burst of sexual activity among viagrafied seniors has come a spurt in HIV cases. If testing sounds outrageous to your man, gently point out that in today's world it's only common sense, and, because it is, you'll take the test, too.

What if, six months later, you catch him cheating? Your first instinct would most certainly be to show him the door and throw his clothes into the street behind him. Who could possibly disagree with that? Not I. It's every wronged woman's right. But consider an alternative – one which you can certainly reject out of hand. I know two women who made the angry woman-scorned decision: "You bastard! You cheated! Get out of my life! I'm divorcing you!" The cheaters remarried. The women never reconnected. They've been more or less miserable for the 30 years since.

So there is a second way. A woman can think of the event, traumatic as it is, as a warning. She can ask herself the questions: "Why did he cheat? What did he need that I failed to give him in our relationship?" She can see a couples therapist with him. Then, if she's convinced that he realizes he made a stupid mistake, has rethought their relationship, and can be trusted, she can offer him a second chance. But, of course, not a third.

Rx No. 36:
Don't be afraid of "intimacy."

I put intimacy in quotes because I'm not talking about sex (well, not yet), but rather a dictionary definition that emphasizes "warm friendship" and "close personal relations." It grows from having the courage to voice inner feelings rather than skating safely on the conversational surface.

You'll know yours is an intimate relationship and not just about satisfying your physical needs, if you feel in a comfort zone when you have to tell him just before you go out to dinner with friends that the jeans and sneakers he's wearing just won't do. And he feels safe informing you that wearing that sweater with the horizontal stripes makes you look ten pounds heavier. Of course, it helps to add, "I'm only telling you because I love you."

But intimate means far more than that, and even more than – if you're a good reader – reading adoration in his eyes. Intimacy and love can be expressed in ways other than with words. "When Will comes to spend the weekend," says Helen, "he gets up before I do and brings me breakfast in bed. He makes me feel wonderful, kind of a queen for the day – and I never asked him to do it. What could be better for a relationship than that?"

Disagreements, even shouting matches, are almost certain to occur because, well, because it's human nature. How you handle them is more important than what they're about, and it's more important to win hearts than arguments. Consider invoking the five-block rule. If you haven't reached a consensus at the end of a five block argument – particularly if you're arguing about something you realize isn't really important – just agree to disagree. Period. Let it go.

But repeated bickering is a sure sign that you've begun an oil and water relationship. Clearly it's better to eat breakfast with the morning paper than with the wrong man. So, if major doubts continue to cling, at some point you have to ask yourself, "Do I really want this creep in my life for the rest of my life?"

If the answer is maybe, work at eliminating the frictions. If the answer is no, it's time to eliminate the man.

Rx No. 37:
Teach him about the birds, the bees, and Viagra.

True story. One of my friends, Sheila, connected with a handsome retired naval officer on the net, and they hit it off immediately. After a few dates and a few drinks, they repaired to his condo to do what comes naturally. Only he couldn't. "Must have been the wine," he said lamely.

Sheila was willing to accept that. This was, after all, a sturdy officer who looked as though he could leap tall battleships at a single bound. Several nights later they tried again. Again he ran up the white flag. This was almost as embarrassing to her as it was to him. He summarily rejected her delicately phrased suggestion that he consider a pharmaceutical solution as harshly as though she'd accused him of giving the Japanese Air Force directions to Pearl Harbor. They terminated their relationship.

To Sheila's surprise, the commander telephoned her several weeks later. "I'm feeling great," he said. "Come on over Saturday night. We'll have a ball. Guaranteed." "Hmm," she thought. "He must have gotten himself a prescription for that little blue tablet." She bought a sexy new negligee, dressed to the elevens, and eagerly presented herself at his door. After a fine dinner accompanied by a single glass of wine, he dimmed the lights and steered her to the bedroom. "But let me make one thing clear," he thundered, raising his head from the pillow, "no Viagra for me!" And then, once again, he proved he needed it.

Naval officers aren't the only males too proud to admit they need reinforcements. Consider this scenario. It's your fourth date and you've decided that it's now or never. You slip into bed with your prospective One and Only. Your lips meet. You embrace with a shiver of anticipation. His hands slide over your body. ("My, they're rough -- I need to teach him about hand lotion.") Yours explore his. ("Ohmigoodness, it's a long time since I touched one of those.")

The foreplay continues, and, after all those years, it's wonderful. But then, to your dismay and even more to his, after several aborted attempts, it's distressingly clear that, for tonight, at least, there will be no ultimate connection. The moment has come and the moment has gone. He has tacitly acknowledged: Emission Impossible.

He's humiliated. If he could find his trousers, he'd gather them up and flee. You're disappointed. If you could, you would cry. Now what? You could dump him with a stern, "Never darken my bedroom again!" As he dresses and slinks out the door, you could rush to your computer, click to your dating site, check out the day's computer matches, and start the dating game all over again.

But you really like this guy. So when he fizzles instead of sizzles, hide your disappointment, smile understandingly, and comfort him in his hour of humiliation. Be loving, reassuring, compassionate, and make another date for which he is to bring Viagra (or Cialis or Vietra) instead of roses. Of course, for those who visit their cardiologist regularly for cardiac problems or high blood pressure, none of those pharmaceutical erector sets is an option. But all lust is not lost. His urologist can prescribe an injection or The Pump, which creates a vacuum to draw blood into his member and magically firms it.

For a lover in otherwise good health, become a friendly urology consultant. Press his head to your bosom and say tenderly, "You know, a little Viagra goes a long way." Then rush on before, machismo offended, he can snort, "Never!" Quickly tell him, in words akin to these: "Doctors recommend and prescribe it. Unless you have a heart condition or high blood pressure, there are absolutely no side effects. Why, even 20- and 30-year olds are using it -- to enhance performance. When a man reaches his 50s and 60s, the major supply blood vessel often starts to occlude. Viagra and similar products open up that passage and, if the woman you're with turns you on, an excellent erection follows. Long-lasting, too. Tell you what. Get a prescription from your doctor, and I'll meet you back here same time same station tomorrow night."

Or words to that effect. Hey, if you really like the guy, you'll want to help him.

And yourself.

Rx No. 38:
Don't keep what you're thinking a secret

Unless the man you're dating is from Venus instead of Mars, the delicate subject of sex -- in the city or the suburbs -- is bound to come up. He may be Bogart-direct ("Look here, Doll, it's time we hit the sack!") or Fonda-subtle ("Isn't it time we spent some intimate time together?") Either approach, particularly early in your relationship, could tempt you to say, "Sayonara" to a man you had begun to think might be the man for you.

When it happened to Elsie on their third date, her response was an indignant, "What kind of woman do you think I am?" She had mixed feelings, a lot of them very positive, but she refused to continue a relationship with a man she quickly concluded was hot for her body, not her heart. Maybe too quickly. Communications failure.

What she should have done was sit him down, as far from the bedroom as possible, for a thoughtful one-on-one, beginning with something like: "George, I'm just not ready. It's not that I don't like sex. It's not that I don't like you. It's that I need to know you a lot better." If George wants a time-table, there's always, "Soon." Or, "After a while." If that's not good enough, it's time to show him to the nearest exit. When you've finally granted him permission to head for the boudoir instead of the door, it's time to forthrightly push the communications button. What makes you feel good is just as important as what makes him feel good. So tell him. And afterwards tell him (assuming there's some truth to it), "You really are a wonderful lover." That's a welcome compliment to any man. And if he says, "Aw, shucks," you add, "But I know how to make you even better." You'll have done both of you a sterling service.

Widow Bernice was number 20 on a list of 41 responses widower Murray got to his "man seeking woman" newspaper classified ad. Murray, going about his search methodically, had dated two women every week. He liked Bernice on the first date, and she liked him. He made an exception to his no-second-date (not yet anyway) policy, and they enjoyed the second time even more. But then Murray announced his intention of continuing down his list at his previous two-a-week pace. After that, he'd be back. Maybe.

That night, Bernice thought that over. Next day she phoned him. "I do like you," she said, "and I enjoyed our time together. But I'm uncomfortable with your seeing all those other women. We've gone out twice. If that didn't do it, then don't bother coming back. I won't want to see you again."

Now it was Murray's turn to think things over. Bernice, he decided, was special. It was hard to put his list aside, but reluctantly, shelve it he did. He'd found an honest, intelligent, and attractive companion who was not afraid to say what she thought. What more could he want? They've been together ever since. Eight very loving years.

There have, of course, been less than happy moments. "I have to admit," admits Murray, "there were a few times that troubled me. I agreed that we should do everything together – going to the movies, to an opera, to dinner, and, in fact, to keep the calories down, we often share a dinner. But, at the same time, sometimes I felt a little smothered. Like I'd feel like lying down on the couch to take a nap, but Bernice was in the mood to talk politics. Situations like that came up now and then, and I didn't want to hurt her feelings. So we talked it out. Or, as they say today, we communicated. The results were excellent. We agreed that it's silly to think we have to hold hands every moment. Now if I want to take a mid-day swim, or she wants to lie down on the couch and read the paper, we respect each other's freedom. We can each do our thing with no one feeling injured, whereas if we'd swallowed our feelings, it could have choked our relationship."

Unlike Bernice, Betty needed help with her communication skills. On e-mail and the phone, Victor seemed an interesting candidate, but Betty's first date with him was a turn-off from the moment they sat down at their restaurant table. Without so much as a, "Would you like anything special?" Charlie picked up a menu and proceeded to order for both of them. On the second date, he chose the movie without consulting her. On the third, it was a show. "It was as though," said Betty, "he came out of a cave and had slept through the entire Women's Lib movement. When he called for a fourth date, I just told him I was busy."

"Why didn't you just tell him what you were thinking each time?" I asked her.

"Oh," she replied, "I didn't think it was polite to object."

Possibly Charlie was born a control freak. Or maybe he'd had a wife who couldn't make up her mind and let him make all the decisions. In any case, rather than bounce her beau, Betty could have said something as simple as, "Charlie, I think it's kind of sweet that you surprise me by choosing our dinners and movies. But, you know, I'm a big girl and I have a mind of my own. So on dates from now on, how about we decide things 50-50? What do you say?"

He'd almost certainly say, "I apologize. It's consensus decisions from now on." Anything else and it would be time to bid him adieu and go back to the computer drawing board.

Fran and Harvey are another case in point. When they agreed to move in together, she had no idea that he was the kind of pre-Betty Friedan caveman who dropped dirty socks and underwear on the floor expecting her to pick them up and return them to him washed and spotless. The more she surrendered, the more he demanded. Fortunately, Claire, her daughter and confidante, was not happy with the situation and suggested that she take a course in Assertiveness Training at a local community college. It changed her life. Harvey's, too. "Put them in the hamper and they'll get washed" was what she said. "Sometimes by me. Sometimes by you. I'll teach you."

It's never a good idea to keep your mouth shut "to avoid an argument." Recent studies warn that swallowing your feelings is bad for your health – so bad that women who do that regularly risk taking as much as five years off their lives. As a form of communication, arguing – at any rate, discussing heatedly – is absolutely necessary. You might think of an argument as the hot iron that helps "iron out" differences between two people who, unless cloned, couldn't possibly be alike.

Think about it. All day long we have to be nice to our bosses, to our neighbors, to the bank teller, the nanny, the housekeeper, the in-laws. We need someone we can safely "get mad at." If it's someone we can kiss and make up with afterward, we're way ahead of the game.

BLANKET COVERAGE

It's not so bad to sleep alone
No one to steal your cover.
But wouldn't you forgive
Your lover?

Rx No. 39:
Don't do him any boudoir favors. Yet.

When is a matter of opinion, and there are many opinions. One is that of my friend, Renee, who, you may remember, advertised that she had "no objection to sex." You may not want to be quite that out-front. You'll probably prefer to tell the over-eager beaver who tries to talk you into being a First Nighter that you're not the type who goes to bed on a first date. Maybe, "Sorry. I'm not like a car you can take out for a spin the first time you see it in the showroom." But leave him with some hope for the future.

This is, of course, a much bigger problem for 20- and 30-somethings. There are all kinds of unwritten rules among young sex-in-the-city types. Like never on the first date – but never say never. And sex on the second date's okay because if you hold out for the third date, there may not be a third date.

My own feeling is that you should be friends before you're lovers, and rather than follow 30-Something rules, you should make your own – whatever makes you comfortable. In any case, don't invite him into bed because you fear he's getting impatient and you'll lose him. For heaven's sake, have confidence in yourself. If all he wants is a roll in the linens, he's not the guy for you anyway.

Carla learned that the hard way. She had gone through a painful divorce, and on her 50th birthday woke up with a feeling she didn't like one bit -- that life was passing her by faster than a police squad car in hot pursuit. Carla decided that it was time to get into the fast lane. She booked dates on the internet, out of newspaper personals, with men she met at coffee shops, and in fix-ups from friends' divorced cousins. They were happy to oblige, and she went to bed with one and almost all.

One morning she awoke with a different feeling: itching in and around her vagina. Herpes -- which she learned when she visited her gynecologist, would be with her for the rest of her life. End of wild sex. Possibly the end -- if she was honest and didn't want to infect another partner – of any sex. Permanently.

Beth was luckier. The wonderful man she'd had a wonderful -- but sex-free – evening with called her the next day. "I had a great time last night," he said. "So did I," she replied warmly. "But there's something I have to tell you." He paused. Beth bit her lip. He was married? He had cancer? His company was transferring him to Tokyo? "I have to be honest," he said. "I like you too much to be anything else. I hope it's not going to be the end of our relationship, but...I have herpes."

"I like you a lot, too," Beth said after a long moment. "But I don't know all I need to know about herpes. Before I say anything more, I'd like to ask my doctor's opinion." She did, and his advice came immediately. "Herpes is no joke," he said. "Sores and scabs from the genital area to the anus. And it's highly contagious. He made a mistake. You don't have to. Drop him. Now." Beth did.

Doctors can be wrong, but here we have a classic case of, "Doctor knows best." And I think not a single physician in the AMA would disagree with this: "Before you go to bed with a man, tell him he's got to go to the doctor for a complete blood test first. If he won't, you don't. Instead, play the waiting game. Until you meet the right man. Until he's certified. Until he turns you on. Until, perhaps, walking through the park with your hand in his, you suddenly feel warm all over, and you think, wouldn't it be wonderful if all the lonely women in the world could feel this good, and now, yes now, you know you want his head on the pillow beside yours. And now, yes now, the time has suddenly become riper than a Florida orange grove in January. So: not the first date, not the second, but whenever it feels right.

AIDS SERMON

Consider this before you bed
While you're still fully clad
When making love you're coupling with
Each mate your partner's ever had.

Rx No. 40:
Conquer your fear of trying.

If sex fails to live up to your expectations the first time, grin and bear it. Don't be surprised, and, even more important, don't fear that's the way it's always going to be. Rome wasn't burned in a day. (Just ask Nero.) Expect a period of adjustment, of learning what makes your partner's heart sing, and yours. To lubricate or not to lubricate is sometimes the question.

After years without sex, some of us need to be treated as gently as a vestal virgin on her honeymoon. Any gynecologist will tell you that for some women vaginal secretions that once flowed like Saudi oil wells when they so much as looked at a hunk become dry wells when they reach menopause-plus. The hormone factory has long since closed down and the resultant dryness could result in ow's instead of ooh's.

Stella can vouch for that. We met the other day, between the first and second acts of an off-Broadway show when I asked, "How do you like the show so far?" (She didn't.) Somehow that segued into a discussion of her sex life. (Don't ask me how. It just did. As usual, I'm afraid I started it.)

"I'm 75," said Stella, who looked 20 years younger. "And I'm 78," said her robust-looking husband, who does two hours of aerobics three times a week. "I'd love to do that good stuff we used to do in bed, but she doesn't want to. She says she's too tired."

"The truth is," said Stella sadly, "it hurts."

Why they both thought there was nothing they could do about I haven't the slightest idea, but ignorance was definitely not bliss. So I explained to her (as a smile brightened her husband's face) it doesn't have to hurt. Love-making at any age, I told her, should be pleasurable, not painful, and a tube of Astroglide or any of a half-dozen other products available over the counter can turn agony into ecstasy.

If not, it's time to turn to a gynecologist for customized assistance. She or he may prescribe something like Vagifem – which, in fact, a close friend of mine calls "miraculous." It ended Marge's fear of trying. Hopefully, it will end Stella's as well.

NIGHT CALL

In bed I hear her sigh
Her meaning's elusive
When I ask she explains
"It's all-inclusive."

Rx No. 41:
Sex is wonderful, but it isn't everything.

Lovemaking (a.k.a. sex) is more important to a relationship than almost anything else. But someone who, perhaps because of a heart condition, feels over the hill sexually can still be loving and loveable. We all need affection. It's comfort food for body and soul. Lavish it upon him and he'll reciprocate.

That's what Fran, 55, did with someone she dated a half-dozen times, her feelings for him growing stronger each time. "I think," she confided to her sister, "I may have finally found The One." One thing puzzled Fran, but she attributed it to shyness on Tim's part. Unlike some other men she'd gone out with, he made no attempt to steer her toward the bedroom.

When, finally, remarking on it several weeks later, she told him how much she appreciated his being a gentleman but that it was okay to be a bit more forward, suddenly it was confession time. "It's hard to talk about it," he said. "I really like you. I'm starting to love you. But if we're going to continue together, there's something I've got to tell you sooner or later." He rose, walked around the room, and then blurted hurriedly, "I was born with a genetic defect. I can't have normal sex. Now is that okay, or is it all over?"

I wasn't there. I'm just repeating what Fran told me. But I'll bet that Tim's admission was followed by a very long silence. Then she threw her arms around him. "Absolutely not!" she said. "Sex isn't everything. We've had great times together. It's you I love, not your equipment." Enjoying everything but the ultimate connection, they've been together ever since.

Rx. No. 42:
Be very sure before you call the movers.

Personally, I'm not big on X moving in with Y. Too many things can go wrong – and they did for Ellen. After what used to be called "a whirlwind courtship," Barney sold his apartment and moved in with her, but before the year was out, she knew she'd made a very large mistake. It took her another year, during which she hoped the stars would return to her eyes, before she told Barney it might be best if he moved out. A third year passed with his sleeping on the couch, "looking" but not finding a condo he could afford.

And then, like heat lightning on an August night, suddenly and unexpectedly he became seriously ill. A month later, after she'd thought things over, Ellen called his sister. She told her that she'd decided to move to California where her daughter lived and, not unreasonably, asked her to take charge of her brother's care.

There's a wonderful way to avoid that sort of depressing and often guilt-racked situation. You like him. He likes you. He wants to move in, but you're not sure you're ready. A flat no and he could be gone with the wind, so you might consider a trial weekend. On the other hand, moving in may not make the most sense. You'll be more interesting to each other if you have separate lives and interests. And the love spark will glow brighter if he comes on Wednesdays, leaves

Thursday morning, and comes back Friday for a long weekend. An arrangement like that has worked well for several couples I know. Distance makes the heart grow fonder and the libido stronger. And parting isn't such sweet sorrow if, "I'll see you the day after tomorrow."

Marriage? It's always an option, but it's less of an option for seniors than in uncomplicated days gone by. Like a boulder dropped in a pond, it has powerful ripples. You know them as well as I. You could forfeit your late husband's pension and health benefits which belong to you only as long as you're his unwed widow. To women with sizeable bank accounts and investments, that could be unimportant. But it's something to think about.

What will the children think? Well, that's another issue. Unless they're independently wealthy saints, they're likely to be uneasy about possible future in-your-dotage rewrites of your will. Millie, an attractive widow in her mid-70s, had reservations at first but quickly came to like the full-service assisted living facility she moved into. She liked it even more when Lowell, a slim dapper retired attorney, a widower with a glitzy sports car, moved into the next suite. They became fast friends. Fast intimates as well. They were inseparable until Lowell's apprehensive children conspired to separate them.

"Millie's after your money," they announced at every opportunity. "She's a 75-year-old gold-digger. They made their dislike so clear that, for the sake of family harmony, Lowell regretfully moved to another condo. Millie had lived long enough to take it philosophically. "It's probably a good thing," she said. "I was getting fat drinking wine with Lowell and pigging out on hors d'oeuvres before dinner."

Well, kids will be kids. My friend, Ted, wrote his daughter a letter 25 or so years ago gently questioning the morality of her plan to move in with her boyfriend. Now, having learned that her father has moved in with a lady love of his own (and laughing so hard she could hardly see her computer screen) his daughter has written the same letter to him. Only hers ends, "But more power to you, Dad!"

The Forever After Rx

Finding Mr. Almost Perfect is hard enough. Keeping the relationship from going stale is sometimes harder. I give you Shelly, who has been married for 33 years to the same man, but is a prime example nevertheless.

"Shirley," she confided one day, "I heard you counseling Phyllis about sex and I am very upset. Maybe you can help me." She lowered her voice to a whisper: "We sleep in twin beds. And I haven't had sex with my husband for seven years."

Knowing Harold, I knew why. Shelly had been poisoning their relationship a lot longer than that. Men need support and the occasional compliment every bit as much as we do. She criticized instead. She had gained a great deal of weight, wore dowdy clothes, had let herself go, and, not surprisingly, the fun and laughter of their early years had gone out of their marriage.

"Shelly," I told her, "you've been doing all the wrong things – things that keep a man from loving a woman and being proud of her. First of all, you've got to stop being so critical and start being loving – surprising him with little treats and kindnesses. You've got to lose a little weight and then buy a sexy nightgown. Push the two beds together and get aggressive. Touch him. Kiss him. Say you can't live without his love. Warm him up. Get his temperature rising. He'll take it from there."

A few weeks later, Shelly came in with a big smile on her face. "We did it! We did it!" she said. She handed me a Macy's gift certificate. "Here," she said, "I wanted to thank you."

Will Shelly's good fortune continue? Only if she continues to work at it. It's very simple. You have to give in order to get.

YOU MUST REMEMBER THIS

We're all living longer
And that means more fun
Playing bridge
Playing tennis
Maybe finding someone.

Someone you can talk to
Who's gentle and kind
If he's a great lover
I'm sure you won't mind.

For each Jane there's a Jim
For each her a him
You just have to know how to look.
For every Louise
A half-dozen he's
And that's why we've written this book.

--Shirley and Howard

AUTHOR! AUTHOR!

SHIRLEY FRIEDENTHAL could have inspired the song, "Matchmaker, Matchmaker." For 27 years, in her late husband's internal medicine practice, she counseled patients with sexual, marital, and assorted other family problems, occasionally matchmaking on the side. She strengthened her skills with courses in human sexuality, group therapy, and psychology at The New School and New York University, and studied Rational Therapy with Albert Ellis. "That was all about making people happier," Shirley explains. "So is this book."

HOWARD EISENBERG has written for TV, radio, national magazines, and the theatre. Six previous books include two best-sellers – "How to be Your Own Doctor (Sometimes)" and "The Recovery Book" – as well as a college health textbook, and, most recently, the baseball memoir, "A Funny Thing Happened on the Way to Cooperstown." Why is he so sure that it's never too late to date? He and Shirley met on a dating web site five years ago, and they've been OO's (One and Only's) ever since.